THE GREEN LANES OF ENGLAND

THE GREEN LANES OF ENGLAND

Valerie Belsey

"The line, the shadow is always there, even if you can't see it or it isn't entirely apparent."—Andy Goldsworthy, talking about the British landscape in 1997

GREEN BOOKS

First published in 1998
by Green Books Ltd
Foxhole, Dartington
Totnes, Devon TQ9 6EB

Distributed in the USA by
Chelsea Green Publishing Company
White River Junction, Vermont

Typeset in Janson Text
at Green Books

Book design by Rick Lawrence

Printed in Spain
by Grafo S.A., Bilbao

A catalogue record for this book is
available from The British Library

ISBN 1 870098 69 2

CONTENTS

ACKNOWLEDGEMENTS

Firstly I would like to thank all the county councils that responded to my enquiries, as their responses provided the basis of this book; and Modbury Local History Society, who have supported my interest in this subject over the years and were kind enough to sponsor me in this venture.

Looking back to the beginnings of my interest in green lanes, I owe a lot to my employers and employees on the MSC Green Lanes Project; Devon County Council Environment Service and Highways Department; and particularly the Coast and Countryside Service in South Devon for their continuing support for my enthusiasm.

It would be impossible to list all those individuals who have helped in my field studies. Some of them I met in the middle of nowhere, as they were fellow enthusiasts following the same lanes; some were people who just used a lane for their daily walk, and never realized how much they knew about it until they started talking to me. Many thanks, whoever you were! I am also grateful to those who have written to me with additional information over the many years of my interest in the subject.

I would also like to thank the following for supplying information and photos which have been used in this book: Mr. Pattenden of the Cleveland and Teesdale Local History Society, for information on local Enclosure Acts; Peter Rowe of Cleveland Archæological Unit; Cheshire County Council for information on Lambert's Lane; The Coast and Countryside Service, South Hams District Council, for permission to reproduce the Parish Map of Staverton on page 27; Chris and Janet Mitchell for the map of Fishcheater's Lane in Totnes on page 108; Steve Taylor, who provided the illustrations on pages 72 and 121; and the following for photographs reproduced: Helen Davies, page 124 (left); East Sussex County Council, page 92 (right); Tony Gill, pages 20 (foot), 95 (2nd from foot) and 126; Michael Guest, pages 43, 51 (right), 68 and 114; Kate Mount, pages 17, 67 and 124 (right); Susanna Stage, page 108 (right); and Nigel Wellings, pages 84 and 101.

Thanks to my family and friends who have done their best to keep me off the motorways. And finally I would also like to thank my editor, John Elford, for his patience—and for innumerable pots of green tea.

Valerie Belsey
Dartington
March 1998

FOREWORD

by Michael Dower

The English countryside is full of surprises: gifts which can delight those who choose to stop and stare. Its appeal lies in its intricacy and variety, the pattern of "Landscape plotted and pieced—fold, fallow and plough", celebrated by Gerard Manley Hopkins.

That pattern changes swiftly as one moves across country from one parish to another. The flowers, the trees, the buildings change, reflecting the underlying rocks—chalk, greensand, limestone, sandstone, granite—whose colourful lines are packed so close across the geological map of England. The landscape contains, and reveals, a mixture of nature and of artefact arising from millennia of human use of the land.

In this intricate, evolving mechanism of the countryside, green lanes have a special place, because they are both the key and part of the lock.

The key. Take a green lane as your route to traverse the countryside, and you will have both a way and a means of penetrating the character of the place. The sunken lanes or hollows take you, treading on mud or bedrock, to the level of the badger and the roots of great trees, provoking (in summer) Andrew Marvell's "Green Thought in a Green Shade". By contrast, the great drove roads across northern hills, such as Mastiles Lane in the Yorkshire Dales, offer wide views over windswept grazing-lands, with the curlew calling. In the 'bocage' of middle England, green lanes form a charmed avenue, from which five-bar gates open into cow-rich fields and acres of arable land. All green lanes offer the pleasure of movement, sequence, novelty and surprise.

The lock. At the same time, green lanes are a touchstone of what man and God have made together. Each green lane is a precious package of nature and culture—hedges, walls, fences or ditches on each side; verges of greenery, often rich in the flowers special to that area; and the ground, hard or soft, under foot or under hoof. It is a feature of, and a route through, the landscape.

Many green lanes are hundreds of years old, evocative of the past, imbued with the passage of generations of men and women, children and animals, drovers, soldiers, priests and rogues, horsemen, merchants, pack-ponies, sheep, cattle, carts and tractors. Their structure may be modest and anonymous, but they merit the respect that we devote to our churches and cathedrals.

Crossing the countryside, they are corridors also for wildlife, harbour for the finch and the fieldmouse, for the jay and the jack-in-a-hedge, for milkmaid and meadow cranesbill. Where intensive farming has wiped much of the wildlife off the fields, such corridors are precious for the health of wild things. For this reason, too, green lanes merit our protection.

Many of the purposes, such as droving or pilgrimage, for which green lanes were made—or simply appeared through habitual use—have passed into history. As a consequence, the lanes themselves have been neglected, forgotten and in many lengths destroyed. But now a new pattern of use has appeared which may justify a new oiling of the key, a de-rusting of the lock. That new use is the leisure, and the pleasure, of the people.

Green lanes offer a resource for walking, cycling horse-riding, and sometimes for trailriding with motorcycles or for four-wheel-driving. But those who wish to pursue such use must face the captivating, sometimes infuriating, complexity of the English law of highways. Almost always, a green lane is privately owned, and the ownership will change along its length. The public's right of passage along it may be nil, or limited, or complex. It may be a public footpath, or a bridleway, or a road used as a public path, or a by-way open to all traffic.

Such elusive variety is part of the charm, and the local distinctiveness, of the countryside. But it hampers our collective ability to use appropriately, and to care for, this special part of our heritage. A strong case can be made for greater recognition of our remaining green lanes, even for a national register of them. Such bureaucratic formality must, however, be accompanied and tempered by affection and care at local level.

I salute Valerie Belsey as a tenacious champion of green lanes. The strength of her book is that it will provoke understanding, and nurture care, for this precious part of England's heritage.

Michael Dower CBE was Director of Dartington Amenity Research Trust 1967 to 1985, and in that capacity oversaw the study of Green Lanes (carried out for the Countryside Commission), of which some results are quoted in this book. From 1981 to 1985, he was also Director of the Dartington Institute, whose subsidiary the Bridge Community Programme Agency launched the green lanes project in the South Hams. He then served as National Park Officer of the Peak District National Park (1985 to 1992) and as Director General of the Countryside Commission (1992 to 1996). He is now Professor of Countryside Planning at the Cheltenham and Gloucester College of Higher Education, and Secretary General of ECOVAST, the European Council for the Village and Small Town.

Chapter One

WHAT IS A GREEN LANE?

Many a road and track
That since the dawn's first crack,
Up to the forest brink,
Deceived the travellers
Suddenly now blurs
And in they sink.

From *Lights Out* by Edward Thomas

Although there are difficulties in defining the term, the reality of the existence of 'green lanes' seems to grow in our subconscious even as the lanes themselves diminish in number. This may be because, with the rise of the environmental movement, the adjective 'green' has changed so much in meaning over the past fifty years that we now take phrases in which it is used and redefine them for ourselves. A fierce spirit of independence, especially in country dwellers, keeps the adjective 'green' alive and full of symbolic meaning.

In my travels during the research for this book I have come across many paths, tracks and roads described as 'green lanes'. Most are now anything but green—I think in particular of the famous one in Ilford which leads into London. Sometimes they are referred to as green because they are not used much any more (and are literally green with a covering of grass); some of these are considerably older than the roads we use to pass them by. The Icknield Way and the Ridgeway are prehistoric in origin, and although we do not drive along them any more I would say that they are still thoroughfares.

Would it matter to the millions of motorists if green lanes were to disappear forever from our landscape? After all, we have lost far more prominent features in the name of progress: many a prehistoric monument that has stood in the way of a road development has been sliced through. Perhaps there is nothing wrong in that, for although such sites were sacred to our ancestors, they are no longer regarded as such. They were constructed to inspire awe and worship; the monuments and the roads leading up to them were revered by our forebears who, through agriculture and seasonal migrations, changed the face of the land on a seasonal basis. But now, encased in our metal bullets, we shoot through ancient landscapes at all times of the year, no longer making pilgrimages to these ancient sites.

Green lanes have been treated in a similar way, so why do they evoke a stronger reaction in people, when we talk of their destruction? It is surely because, having long ceased worshipping the land and its seasonal patterns, we now worship the act of travelling through the land—and seeing as much of it as we can, whenever we want, at our own frantic and fretful pace. Green lanes belong to another age of travel, and in only a very few cases still serve any significant contemporary purpose. They are a burden to the highways authorities, a restriction on farmers expanding their fields, a danger for children playing on their own.

So why has this book been written? Why does the term 'green lane' still haunt us? It is because we believe

LEFT: Green lanes often lie hidden in the landscape: a lane runs through the middle of the picture, between the two overhanging trees.

in the ghosts of the past. So before we get down to recording the sitings of these ghosts, let us make a definition of the ideal conditions under which they may appear.

There are one or two official definitions which seem to cover all the physical characteristics of green lanes, and they are as follows.

The Countryside Commission

A green lane is best defined in broad general terms, viz. that it is an unmetalled track which may or may not be a right of way for the public either on foot, horse, bicycle or motor vehicle, including a motor bicycle, and which is usually bounded by hedges, walls or ditches (1979).

East Sussex County Council

An unmetalled linear feature bounded on both sides by hedges/banks/ditches, with an appropriate history. Variable width. May be public right of way, designated by 1968 Countryside Act as byway, bridleway, or footpath.

The Dartington Institute Study on Green Lanes

An unmetalled road bounded on either side which may or may not be a right of way and which once was used for a variety of purposes but now is mainly used for recreation (1985).

The degree to which local authorities have undertaken studies and surveys of green lanes in their area varies considerably throughout the country. Lincolnshire has made a particular study of green lanes, and other counties such as Essex and Kent have developed a policy towards minor roads, lanes and green lanes which will ensure their future protection. All have their

Signposting of green lanes can take many forms.

own definitions of a green lane which rely on the physical and legal status of lanes, but there is another quality, which lies in their essential 'greenness'.

There is already a plethora of acronyms which describe them, including BOATs (Byways Open to All Traffic), RUPPs (Roads Used as Public Paths), and UCs (Unclassified roads); nevertheless here is another, which I believe encompasses the ideas which we have about green lanes, both physically and in our imaginations: it is GRUTH—a Green Route Used Throughout History. This is a simple description, which answers many of the questions about their existence which puzzle us. Some truncated sections of lane which exist today seem impossible to envisage as part of any route at all, but that is because our reasons for moving from one place to another have changed so dramatically. In the past we travelled from necessity, but now we have created travel as an activity in itself, an item of conspicuous consumption.

If we forget the 'green' dimension, what is a lane anyway? Today we use the term quite readily when talking about motorways (at one time we were threatened with a twelve-lane version of the M25). A lane implies some kind of restriction on either side, whether it be white lines or whitebeams. Ancient trackways did not need to be contained in this way, and there are still today stretches of the Ridgeway and the Icknield Way which are very wide in places, thus emphasizing their essential 'wayness'. Lanes were not only to be found in the country, but they always seem to have some connection with it—and often retain this in their adjectival definers when they lead into towns and cities. In the City of London, once the home of markets other than financial ones, we still find these rural and trade terms persisting: Honey Lane, Cock Lane, Finch Lane, Carter Lane, Drover Lane, Lamb Lane, Moor Lane, Oat Lane, Coppermill Lane, Coopers Lane—all indicating purposeful traffic towards a city.

Take an old map of any city that you know and study the pattern of the roads which then led into it; you will invariably find a lane whose name describes its original purpose. This original use will almost certainly no longer apply, and changes in local settlement patterns will have occurred; if the road has not been incorporated into the contemporary system of traffic entry into the city, it will have become (or remain) a green lane.

A typical green lane tunnel.

Before I started work on this book, I believed that in my research I would find a greater variety of green lanes than I did in fact discover. This was somewhat disappointing; yet what I discovered in each county reflected

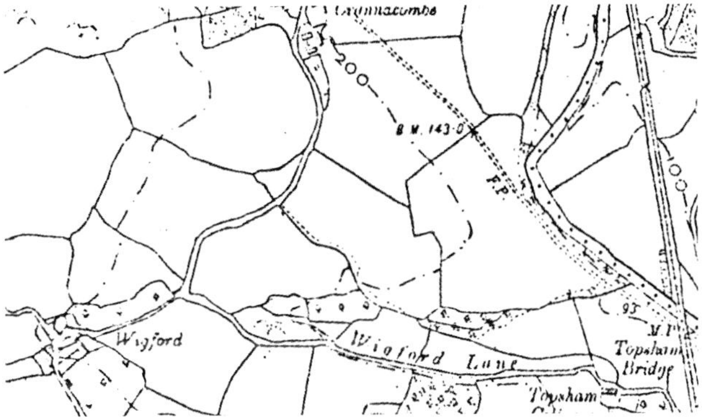

A 1906 OS map showing Wigford lane, with no indication as to its status. On today's map the lane is shown as a broken green line, indicating that it is a public right of way—but if it had not become one, it would still be a green lane.

the subtle differences in landscape which characterize the variety of the English countryside, and it is in this subtlety that all will be lost or found. Every motorway and major road today has a depressing sameness about it: traffic engineers have given us trouble-free roads, with very little concession (although this has improved in the past few years) to the actual shape of the landscape through which we are travelling. Hills have been cut in half or excavated, valleys spanned by concrete creations defying the laws of gravity. Green lanes, however, were for the most part built around the landscape: the technology was not then available to destroy the countryside in order to achieve human ends.

This similarity between green lanes in no way undermines their importance, but rather brings us back to a

Spring, showing celandines and primroses at the foot of the hedgerow.

Summer's heavy foliage in green lanes is rich with colour.

Treading autumn leaves along a sunken green lane.

Winter's dreariness relieved by bright snow in a green lane.

consideration of their original, local use. Global communication seems superfluous in comparison to the needs of communities, which must be met in order that each may survive in its own place, without all the aimless to-ing and fro-ing which has apparently become so important to us today. The ever new, exciting and different—creates indifference.

If you wish to explore the question "What is a green lane?", the best way to do so is to make a detailed study of road communications in your own area, seeing which old routes now remain green, and finding out why. There is no necessity to go running around elsewhere: what you are looking for lies on your own doorstep, and your doorstep is as good as anybody else's in this respect. I do not want this book to promote another wave of people driving about looking for sensations which already exist in the areas where they live and work; on the contrary, I hope that the book will serve to deepen local awareness of our historic landscape.

One of the difficulties in tracing green lanes (those which are not already designated by local authorities as rights of way) is that we often see them when we're on the move, and cannot stop to investigate them further, because someone is driving on our tail. They are features which go unnoticed: when you start to find them, and develop the technique of glancing sideways when driving, it is too late—your green lane has already gone! But it is important that we acknowledge their existence and value them as a part of our highway heritage. Even if they continue to be unused, they are important features of our development from rural to urban creatures, and in some cases may even be the link which bridges the gap between these two worlds.

PASSABLE PASSAGES

As your journey through this book progresses, you will discover the reasons why green lanes come in various widths. Just as a dressmaker cuts the cloth according to what the user requires, so have green lanes developed according to their users' requirements. Packhorse lanes

This lane, snaking through the landscape, is contained by its ancient hedgerows. RIGHT

Green lanes are easily ignored as you whizz by them when travelling on A and B roads, and even motorways.

need be no wider than the animals and their packs, but a road along which over fifty cattle would pass needed to be considerably wider. In the eighteenth century there were a series of Acts of Parliament known as the Broad Wheel Acts, which attempted to regulate the size of waggon and cart wheels. It is interesting to note that the standard broad-wheeled gauge railway first invented by Brunel copied the standard width between the axles of carts and carriages throughout the country (four feet six inches), which in turn replicated the axle width of Roman chariots! If you find a lane which fits these measurements you will know that it might have seen such wheeled traffic. The axle width of motor cars today is, similarly, approximately four feet six inches.

GREEN UNDERFOOT

Chapter Five of this book, which discusses the ecological value of green lanes, contains material on hedgerows, one of the two defining features of a green lane—the other being the surface. When the term 'unmetalled' is used, it refers to the tarmac-free surface of a lane. Prior to the tarmac revolution there were many ways of keeping a lane open for traffic, be it human, animal or animal-propelled. A study of a geological map of the area in which you live will reveal the pattern of soil and rocks which determined the course of early roads and how their surfaces were constructed. The illustrations on subsequent pages give some indication of this. I know of no study which has been made to determine the age of some of the surfaces shown: for example, do all cobbled lanes date from the same time, or were there advances in cobbling techniques? The illustrations on page 18 indicate this—or they may just have deteriorated over the passage of time? Some conclusions may be drawn from studying these surfaces in

The width of the lane often corresponds to the width of its entrance.

terms of the construction techniques used, which relate to different historical periods. Prehistoric road-builders apparently made no attempt to treat the surfaces over which they moved, but the Romans were consummate engineers in this respect; the section of road between Badbury and Salisbury illustrates this in great detail.

The road was built across dry chalkland but, unlike the Ridgeway and the Icknield way, the Romans

This green lane has a metalled surface but access is restricted to residents only, a characteristic which makes it more likely to become green over the years. RIGHT

An impacted Roman road surface.

Cobbled way leading to a church.

A green lane with a green surface.

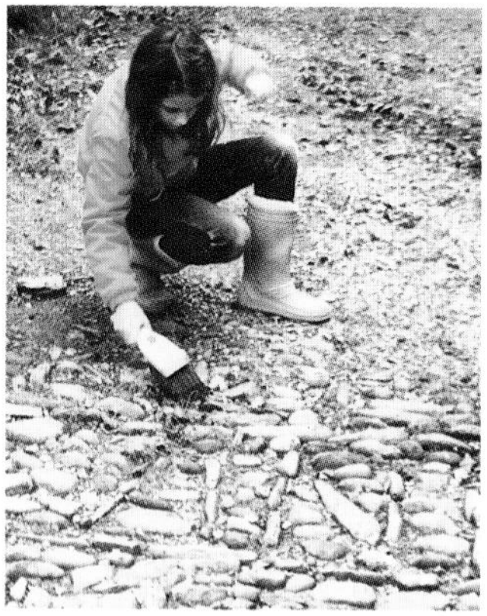

Initials picked out in cobbles of a different colour.

attempted to lift it above the natural level of the surface. They did this by using large banks of flint rammed together with chalk. The surface itself is made of gravel from the quarry at Pentridge.

Road-makers from Anglo-Saxon times onwards obviously made use of whatever materials were at hand, but surfacing seems to have belonged to a post- rather than a pre-mediæval period. Clay was a constant problem, as this story from Aylesbury illustrates.

> In 1499 a glover from Leighton Buzzard travelled with his wares to Aylesbury for the market before Christmas Day. It happened that an Aylesbury miller, Richard Boose, finding that his mill needed repairs, sent a couple of servants to dig clay called 'Ramming clay' for him on the highway, and was in no way dismayed because the digging of this clay made a great pit in the middle of the road ten feet wide, eight feet broad, and eight feet deep, which was quickly filled with water by the winter rains. But the unhappy glover, making his way from the town in the dusk, with his horse laden with panniers full of gloves, straightway fell into the pit, and man and horse were drowned. The miller was charged with his death, but was acquitted by the court on the ground that he had had no malicious intent, and had only dug the pit to repair his mill, and because he really did not know of any other place to get the kind of clay he wanted save the highroad.

Examples of all the different types of surfaces used throughout history are to be found in green lanes (including in some cases remnants of tarmac dating from the 1920s). Then there are those green lanes which are still green underfoot: they seem to awaken our deepest feelings of old England and evoke ideas of travelling with the masons, carpenters, jugglers, mountebanks and thieves who once inhabited them.

Another common feature of a green lane is the fact that it is frequently sunken (these are referred to as 'holloways' or 'hollow ways'—as in the Holloway Road in London). Depending upon the part of the country in which you live, this 'below the field level' status, creating

Heavily eroded lanes can still be dangerous for travellers.

the feeling of being in a green tunnel, can evoke a 'greengood' factor which you will not find in any other means of travel.

When writing this book it seemed a good idea to write up in detail for each historical period a lane which could be walked in each particular area of the country. But I found that many lanes were not in the 'walking along and coming back to where you started from' category, as they had been built with a working purpose. In some instances, the only way such routes could be authentically enjoyed today would be by walking along them for a about a mile or two and then spending the day there, imagining you were ploughing, milling, mining etc., and then walking back again!

STONE WALLING

In the various definitions of green lanes given above, the word 'boundary' occurs. There are many ways in which boundaries can be marked, and many excellent books which deal with the ancient art of stone walling, so only a few examples have been given here (see page 20).

THE HISTORICAL APPROACH

This book has been structured according to the history of highway development in Britain. As a reference point, I suggest that you work from the following historical table:

This atmospheric photograph shows a scene which is apparently timeless, but the road is, in fact, in the process of being destroyed by the building of a bypass.

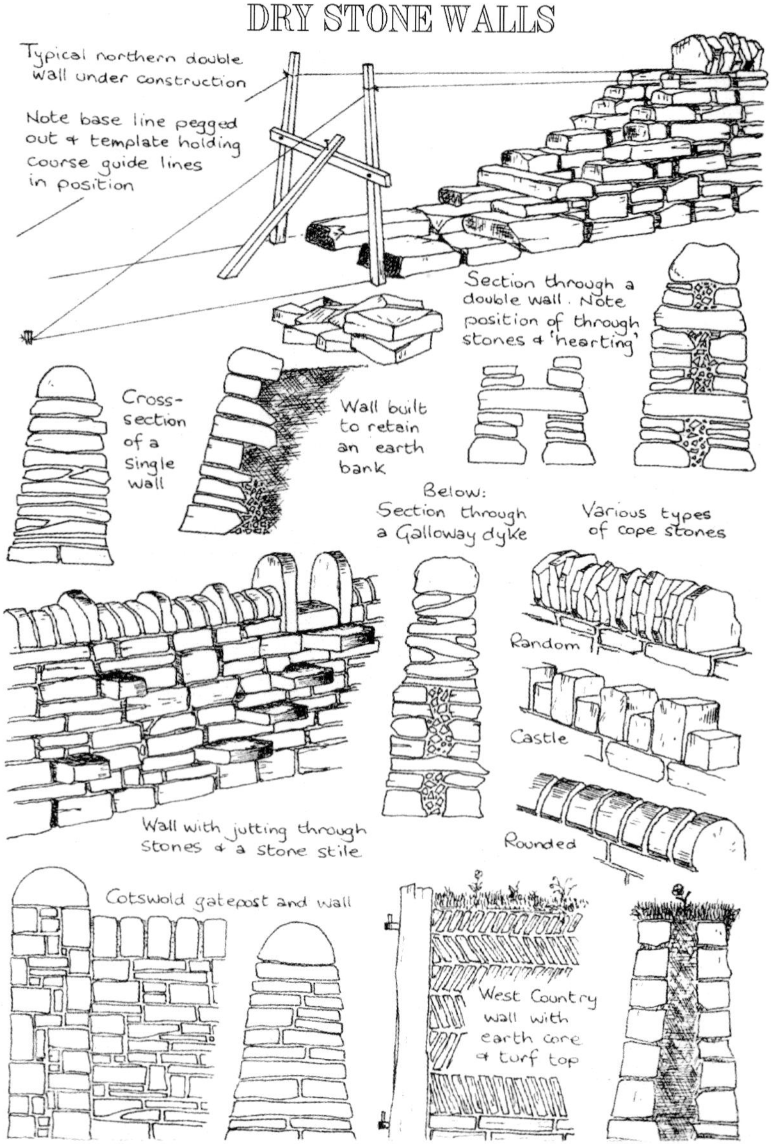
DRY STONE WALLS
Typical northern double wall under construction
Note base line pegged out & template holding course guide lines in position
Section through a double wall. Note position of through stones & 'hearting'
Cross-section of a single wall
Wall built to retain an earth bank
Below: Section through a Galloway dyke
Various types of cope stones
Random
Castle
Rounded
Wall with jutting through stones & a stone stile
Cotswold gatepost and wall
West Country wall with earth core & turf top

1140 Order of King Stephen: Lords of the Manor to keep highways open.

1285 King Edward I's Trench Act: roads through woods were to be 60 feet wide on either side of the King's Way.

1293 Statute of Winchester: all highways from one market town to another were to be enlarged so that there is no dyke or bush within 200 feet on either side (a bow shot).

1531 'C' stones (see below) were put up one hundred yards either side of a bridge.

1536 Bridges were to have parapets three feet or more in height, to deter robbers.

1555 Statute of Phillip and Mary: parishes to maintain roads. There was an elected surveyor and a system of voluntary labour, later amended in...

1563 Elizabeth I: voluntary labour days increased to six per person per year.

1654 The Commonwealth: the Government was given powers to levy a local rate for the construction of roads.

1663 First turnpike (toll-paying road) introduced into this country.

1835 The Highway Act: this established parish and district surveyors, highways boards and jurisdiction of Petty Sessions to levy fines.

1875 The Public Health Act: divided England into Urban and Rural Districts and created Urban Sanitary Districts.

A mounting block at Bisteignton, Devon. These were used by the wealthier members of society to mount their horses without getting their feet muddy.

'C' stones can date from 1531 (see text above).

CONCLUSION

R. Hippisley-Cox, author of *The Green Roads of England*, had this to say about his book (published in 1927):

> The title of my book, is, I fear, more appropriate to its promise than its performance, but short week-ends snatched from other duties have not allowed me time to examine the more distant watersheds. If I can induce others to take their walks along these ancient paths it may be possible in the future to give a fuller account of the Green Roads of England.

And so it is with mine. It will be a disappointment to

those of you who will have hoped that this book would contain some kind of definitive gazetteer of all the Green Lanes of England. But whilst writing it, it has become clear to me that interest in these old ways needs to be pursued at a local level, and that their importance should be re-established in our minds so that they are preserved for future generations to study. Having said earlier that I was initially disappointed at the lack of variety in green lanes, this disappointment has since been tempered by the discovery of pockets of the English countryside which remain so different from each other that they make you feel that you have discovered a new, unexplored landscape—which indeed you have. There has been an upturn in 'green tourism' in recent years, and one of the best ways of getting to know a new area is by setting out to appreciate its landscape through its road patterns. Standing in a disused muddy lane and looking over the hedge into the heart of a particular landscape will often give you the key to its existence far better than exploring the centre of its uniform-looking county town.

Then there is the enormous potential which these lanes have to reveal some little-known history: the disused turnpikes in the Peak District built by 'Blind' Jack Metcalf; the valley at the bottom of a green lane in south Devon where W.B. Yeats and his brother Jack practised black magic; the lane which lured a young girl to a fairy king's palace in Cornwall—the list is endless. And there are the stories which you can make up for yourself, once you know what a lane was used for. You can imagine the merchants on their way to market with vastly different goods to those which are displayed in market towns today; the weariness of the long distance drovers as they reached their markets in London having travelled all the way from Wales and Scotland through green lanes; the desperation of a Saxon farmer urging his ox-team through a clay-bound headland out onto a green lane in early November, whilst looking forward to returning home to his peat fire.

Some green lanes seem to be pathways into unknown territory.

Then there are the strange names that some lanes bear which may give you a clue as to their history, such as Chuckacheese Lane in Stokenham, Devon, or Runaway Lane in Modbury, also in Devon. Is this latter the site of some well-remembered flight from a bull by a local lad? No, its origin is much more historic: the details are given in a later chapter (see page 111). Yet the history of these lanes is often undiscovered, as are the lanes themselves.

For readers with a head for statistics, on page 25 there are figures taken from the Dartington Institute Report concerning the distribution of green lanes throughout the country.

The rough landscapes of Dartmoor and the Peak District reveal in their stony lanes the harsh conditions

This Green Route Used Throughout History (GRUTH) has an evocative quality. RIGHT

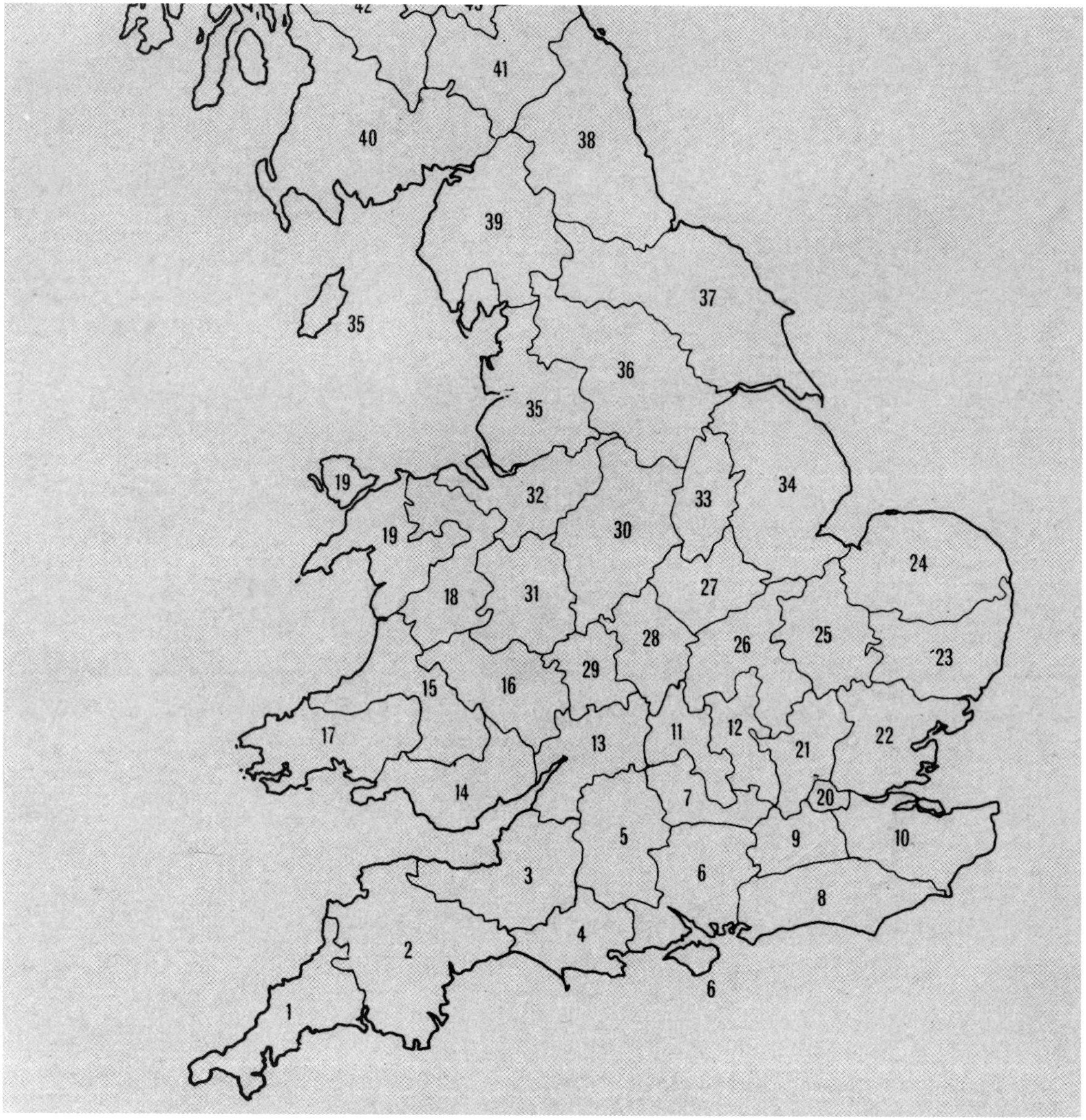

41
40
38
39
37
35
36
35
19
32
34
33
19
30
24
18
31
27
28
26
25
23
29
15
16
17
11
12
13
21
22
20
14
7
5
9
10
3
6
8
4
2
6
1

LENGTH OF PUBLIC ROADS AND PATHS IN THE COUNTIES OF ENGLAND IN 1976 (IN KILOMETRES) AS GIVEN IN ANNUAL RETURNS TO THE DEPARTMENT OF TRANSPORT

Highway Authority & map code	Area (km^2)	Population (1,000s)*	All roads (km.)	Unclassified roads (km.)	Unsurfaced roads & green lanes (km.)**	Footpaths & bridleways (km.)**
Gtr Manchester (35)	1,377	2,730	7,659	5,774	-	-
Merseyside (35)	648	1,621	4,068	3,180	199	421
South Yorkshire (37)	1,562	1,319	4,849	3,347	-	-
Tyne & Wear	540	1,198	3,851	3,021	-	554
West Midlands	900	2,785	6,284	4,759	12	691
Avon (3 & 13)	1,347	914	4,344	2,540	-	-
Bedfordshire (26)	1,236	481	2,119	1,184	80	1,449
Berkshire (7)	1,260	645	2,973	1,668	322	1,610
Buckinghamshire (12)	1,884	496	3,258	1,721	194	1,766
Cambridgeshire (25)	3,412	533	4,405	1,980	222	2,643
Cheshire (32)	2,324	896	5,344	2,943	29	3,014
Cleveland (38)	584	567	1,979	1,494	20	702
Cornwall (1)	3,549	391	7,288	3,537	47	4,728
Cumbria (39)	6,814	474	7,171	3,327	311	7,348
Derbyshire (30)	2,633	888	5,288	2,704	174	4,865
Devon (2)	6,716	921	12,821	6,514	312	4,914
Dorset (4)	2,656	566	4,439	2,343	835	3,690
Durham (38)	2,438	610	3,602	-	-	-
East Sussex (8)	1,797	658	3,402	-	-	-
Essex (22)	3,676	1,398	7,024	3,941	800	6,400
Gloucestershire (13)	2,645	482	4,820	2,311	149	182
Hampshire (6)	3,777	1,422	7,878	4,333	800	3,883
Hereford & Worcs (16 & 29)	3,930	577	7,085	3,358	116	7,932
Hertfordshire (21)	1,635	940	4,194	2,556	— 1,770 —	
Humberside (34)	3,515	847	5,352	2,825	-	-
Kent (10)	3,735	1,435	8,275	4,775	234	7,882
Lancashire (35)	3,042	1,363	7,000	4,324	0	6,000
Leicestershire (27)	2,550	824	4,809	2,501	164	4,192
Lincolnshire (34)	5,890	513	8,379	3,718	236	6,282
Norfolk (24)	5,360	644	8,596	3,917	406	3,558
North Yorkshire (37)	8,315	645	8,883	4,281	697	9,861
Northamptonshire (26)	2,369	488	3,516	1,728	166	2,789
Northumberland (38)	5,037	283	4,814	2,150	21	4,250
Nottinghamshire (32)	2,214	982	4,212	2,445	169	2,701
Oxfordshire (11)	2,609	530	4,030	1,899	64	3,705
Scilly, Isles of	-	2	45	38	1	-
Shropshire (31)	3,493	348	5,455	2,335	109	5,236
Somerset (3)	3,452	399	6,252	2,938	289	6,738
Staffordshire (30)	2,718	985	5,734	3,159	54	4,267
Suffolk (23)	3,810	562	5,981	2,845	111	3,494
Surrey (9)	1,681	994	4,113	2,472	82	3,232
Warwickshire (28)	1,982	468	3,269	1,542	106	2,809
West Sussex (8)	1,993	630	3,456	1,755	190	3,793
Wight, Isle of (6)	381	110	739	347	32	762
Wiltshire (5)	3,483	501	4,639	1,829	727	5,193
TOTAL	**126,969**	**37,065**	**233,694**	**122,358**	**8,480**	**143,536**
AVERAGE	**2,885**	**823**	**5,193**	**2,845**	**229**	**3,879**

* As estimated by the Registrar-General for mid-1973

** Sometimes estimated, or totals for earlier years

- Indicates figure not known

which have led to the land being farmed in a particular way. In the Midlands and East Anglia, the flat fields were broken up by the access routes through them, some of which are still green lanes. Lush, undulating lands in the south-west of England and the borders of Wales still guard secretly their sunken green lanes, where the long way round was always the best. You can often come across a green tangle of lanes in the most unlikely of places close to towns; such time tunnels can set you off exploring in all sorts of directions. As 'carmageddon' approaches, and lorries continue to use minor roads as rat-runs or alternatives to our over-used motorways, we need to protect our 'urban fringe' green lanes, which were once part of our local communication pattern, against the ever-encroaching motor car.

Removing tarmac from a lane, which could now be truly re-classified as green.

As I have emphasized the importance of becoming aware of the green lanes in your own area and of the localized nature of their distribution, I would just like to explain how I came to be writing a book on such a national scale.

My interest in these lanes first began when I was appointed co-ordinator for the Green Lanes Project in 1983. This project was a Manpower Services Commission scheme sponsored by the Dartington Institute. From an understanding of lane history, I progressed to that of roads, and became the Historical Highway Monument Surveyor for Devon. Having written three books on road history, I thought the way ahead for me might lie in another direction. However I was wrong, as I was asked by Modbury Local History Society in south Devon to write a book on green lanes. I thought that this would be straightforward enough, but hadn't anticipated just what the Society were about to ask me to do. There was enough photographic material from the

Children studying the wildlife value of a green lane.

Dartington project alone to fill a book on Devonshire's green lanes but, as you can see, this was not what they had in mind. With great foresight, they thought a book concerning the nature of green lanes throughout England would be a good idea, and with hindsight they were right. I have travelled throughout the country, discovering little enclaves of lanes that still survive despite the onslaught of traffic from all directions.

Despite my obvious enthusiasm for green lanes, I would like to say that this is not a book for 'environmental twitchers'. My aim is not to encourage you to duplicate the journeys which I have made, for you will be able to find in your own green lanes all the history and wildlife that you will learn about in the following pages. Just turn down a green lane near you, think about its past, and resolve to protect its future.

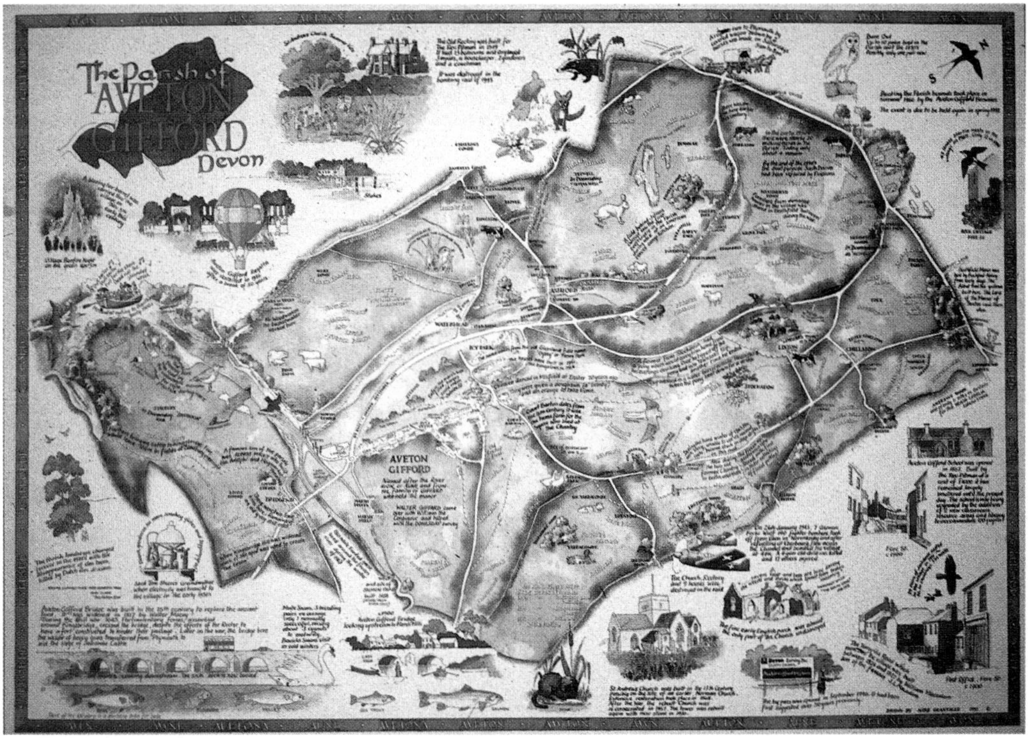

The Common Ground series of parish maps show a modern-day method of recording green lanes.

Chapter Two

THE LONG HAUL

Green Lanes in the Prehistoric & Roman Periods

Suddenly walking along the open road I felt afraid.
I saw the stars and the world below my feet
Become a planet, and I was no longer
In Wiltshire, I was standing
Upon the surface, the edge of a planet
That runs around the sun.
I was in danger.
For all the comfort of the elms, the banal
Normality of houses with their garages, the apparent
Changelessness of the ploughed field on my right—
All was in danger.
A marble spinning through the universe
Wears on its dizzy crust, men, houses, trees
That circle through cavernous æons, and I was afraid.

Mervyn Peake, *Collected Poems*, 1988

Whenever I think back to prehistoric England, it is with a sense of fear: the fear of stepping out onto a highway with no means of knowing where it led to, what you might meet on the way, how long the journey would take, what the conditions would be. It is an odd thing that many of the lanes which are the oldest in England are now the least used. Why, over the hundreds of years of their existence, have they not been tarmacked over and become part of our road network? Some stretches of them have, but there are still large sections of the Icknield Way and the Ridgeway which have their original surfaces, untreated since animals and people first made tracks. It is believed that prehistoric tracks linked burial chambers and religious sites; yet although this is clearly true for Avebury and Stonehenge, it does not necessarily apply elsewhere. Even when such a connection does ring true, as is the case with some of the ley lines plotted by Alfred Watkins in his pioneering book, *The Old Straight Track*, who are we to make such assumptions about our ancestors? Watkins himself realized the danger in this, and questioned whether the lines were “a humanly designed fact, an accidental coincidence, or a mare’s nest”. Much has been written and ‘felt’ about the lines of energy which the leys follow, and my view is that if you want it to be true, it will be for you. We can induce a feeling of treading where our ancestors trod, a literal and metaphorical form of ‘imprinting’.

Most of Watkins’ field work was done on the Welsh borders and in the south of England, so when evidence

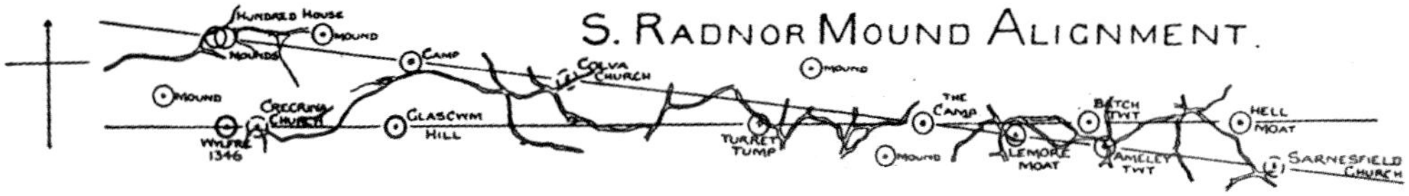

LEFT: A long straight track, typical of the earliest form of green lane: big on width, short on hedgerows.

of a similar nature is found elsewhere it does tend to support the idea that ley lines connect certain prehistoric features. In Staffordshire, John Knox Grave Lane, west of Hopwas (SJ159050), is said to reflect the course of a prehistoric track which linked the Iron Age territory of the tribe of the Coritanii with that of the Cornovii to the west. It is about one and a quarter miles (two kilometres) long and narrows down to a path which links with the later Roman settlement of Letocetum Wall, south of Lichfield. Becoming a lane once more at Stable Lane (SJ117540), it passes some bronze age burial mounds and then some lead mines, before becoming a hedgeless path across the fields. All we can do is look at prehistoric tracks in the light of the difficulties which travel at that period of time must have presented, and assume that our ancestors took the easiest routes between hunting grounds and home.

This chapter is entitled 'The Long Haul' because it seems that wherever prehistoric and Roman roads still survive as green lanes, they have now become long stretches of undeveloped road, which generations have chosen to ignore. Does this mean that in prehistoric times people felt a need to explore that was only indirectly connected with their need to survive—thus proving that we are driven not only by our quest for the basics of life? When we consider lanes from this period on a parochial basis, it is clear that if you had everything you needed within your settlement, you had no need to travel further afield; and yet people did. Man the hunter (women being tied to the prehistoric equivalent of the Aga) firstly followed the tracks of wild animals. Once upon a time these were truly wild, such as sabre-toothed tigers and mammoths; domesticated animals, brought from mainland Europe, followed around 8000 BC. The Icknield Way and the Pilgrim's Way date back to this

The sabre-tooth tiger, which once roamed Britain, was feared and hunted by ancient man.

time. There was also a network of local routes used by wild animals during this period: the domestication of animals such as sheep and horses largely took place between 4000 and 2000 BC. An example of a very early form of drovers' trackway is to be found in Kent: Drake Lane, which follows the old Jutish trackway across the North Downs, just east of Hollingbourne.

Hippisley-Cox's work, *The Green Roads of England* (see page 32), includes maps showing the watersheds in the south of England over which these ridgeways run. There are also other local studies showing watersheds in this area, which are great indicators of early routes (a watershed can either be the raised ground which separates the course of two rivers, or a raised stretch of land between two drainage areas). They are natural features, from which the earliest New Stone Age traders are believed to have developed the long distance routes which followed them, and are easily recognized, as they run along the tops or sides of valleys and are not sunken in any way. They are sometimes referred to as summerways.

An ancient ridgeway in Herefordshire. RIGHT

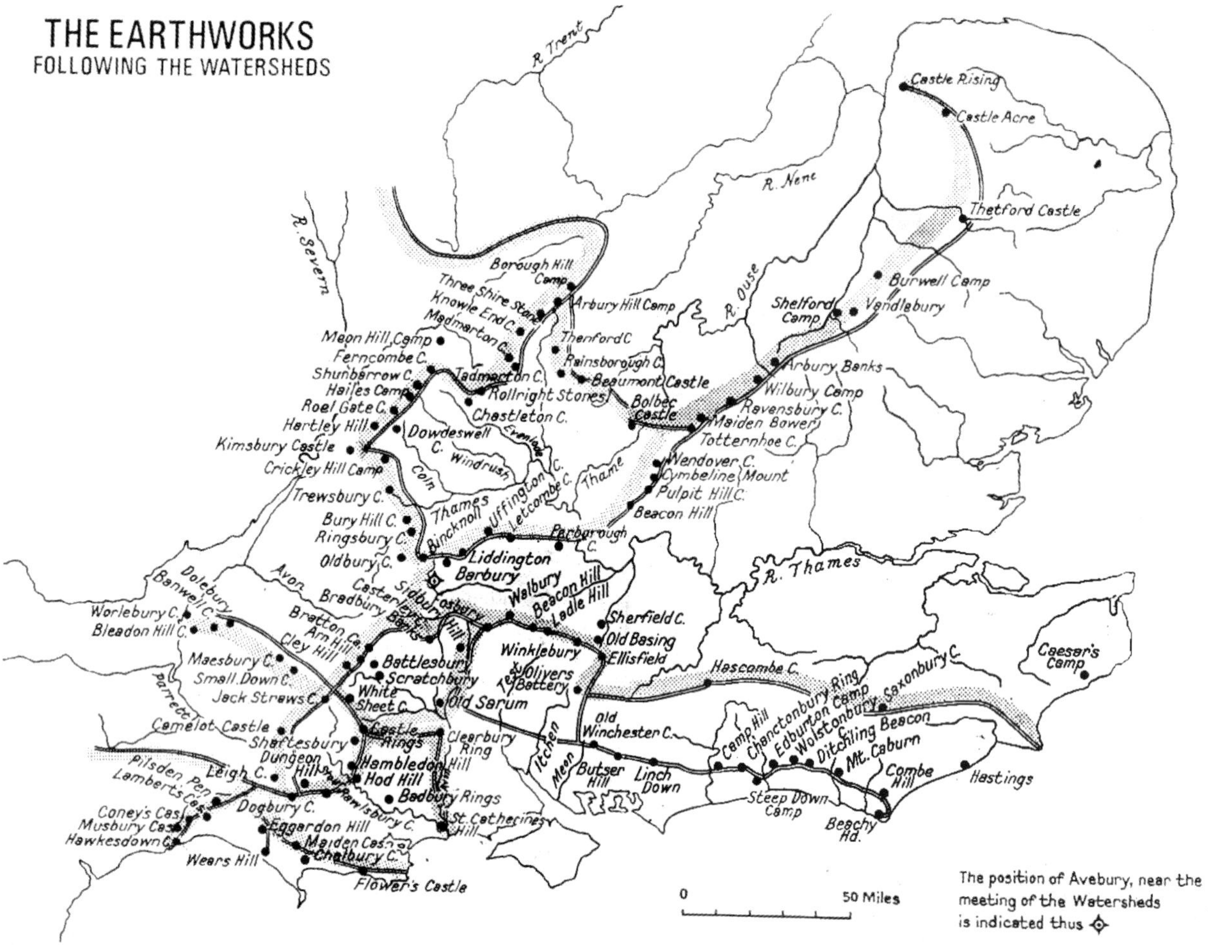

The principal prehistoric trackways which are believed to date from before 2,000 BC. are:

1. The Harroway, from Dover to Cornwall ('harrow' is thought to be a reference to the hardness of the surface).
2. The Ridgeway, from Goring Gap to Salisbury Plain.
3. The Icknield way, which is a northerly extension of the Ridgeway.
4. The South and North Downs Ridgeways.

(Map after Hippisley Cox)

One could add to this list of ridgeways a part of the Jurassic Way, which was conjectured as having run from Lincoln to Glastonbury along high, dry land. A particularly straight section of the route runs south of Moreton Pinkney (SP580477-610507), near Banbury, although some of its straightness owes much to eighteenth century alterations.

The Grundy map (below) shows territory in Devon which is familiar to me, but such ridgeway maps also exist for other parts of the country. This is the case as regards a lane in Herefordshire, known as Macle and Ridge Hill, which leads from Woolhope to Yatton.

Although part of the Pilgrim's Way that lies in Kent was originally a Neolithic way running along the edge of the Downs, there is another route known as 'the greenway' which runs below it. Also in that county there is another route which ran from Kits Coty, avoiding Cranbrook as it made for the River Rother at Newenden.

The basic necessities of life needed to be transported over long distances: salt, tin and maybe rushes to act as tapers. Chert (flint) tools were greatly sought after, and are known to have been carried along long distance routes from Portland in Dorset to Devon, Somerset, Cornwall, Hampshire, the Isle of Wight, Surrey and Gloucestershire. Chert was also transported from Surrey to other parts of England. Flints were delved from the still-wooded green lanes around Grime's Graves near Thetford and delivered to many distant destinations throughout Britain. Examples of the hand axe, for which the best materials were taken from Cumbria, have also been found in many parts of Britain. The hand axe is now used as the symbol for the modern Icknield Way path, which passes through the edges of the Fens in Cambridgeshire and Norfolk, and the valleys of the Debden, Orwell, Stour and Colne rivers in Essex.

The most common form of transport before the invention of the wheel was the sledge. Around 2000 BC, the discovery of metal brought about modifications in sledge design. Green lanes were used from this period

Grundy's Ridgeway map of south Devon.

Prawle, the area on the south Devon peninsula opposite Portlemouth.

Truckamuck.

Hillfort terraces have sometimes developed into sunken green lanes.

onwards (and in some remote cases, up until the mid-1930s in rural areas of Britain) by forms of sledge, hauling timber and building materials about the countryside. These became known as 'truckamucks', which graphically describes their purpose. The resulting erosion of the tracks by the sledges led these primitive hauliers to create parallel tracks, such as on the Icknield Way at Goring.

Traders' resting places developed around what are believed to be prehistoric religious sites. At Maiden Castle in Dorset, the Fosse Way crossed the coastal track from the mines of Cornwall. To reach Hambledon Hill, another trading site, those who journeyed from the south-west must have traversed the present lanes which link the modern villages of Ibberton, Okeford and Shillingstone. Hambledon Hill is also known as a causewayed camp, which reinforces the idea of it having been used by travellers as a safe route—one which was raised above the level of the difficult territory through which it ran.

Green lanes which lead to religious sites are not difficult to find: often they are just short approach roads to the sites in question. One of the more sophisticated sites is to be found in Northumberland, where there is a system of roads leading into the hill fort at Lordenshaws (NZ054993). Some of these roads are stone-faced, and one leads to a spring. At Old Oswestry in Shropshire (SJ296310), the approach road is 16 1/2 metres (54 feet) wide. In Hertfordshire at Ravenburgh Castle (TL099295), it is 150 metres (160 yards) long and the south exit leads to a spring.

Where excavations along prehistoric lanes have occurred, it has usually been more by accident than design. There is much we still do not know about their patterns of use after the prehistoric period. But imagine the Romans arriving on our shores: did they get out their shovels and start building a completely new road network in such a cold climate? Not likely. The invaders used and developed much of the existing prehistoric road network.

Not a typical-looking Roman road. This one in Suffolk is grassed over, having survived as a short cut to the church in the distance. RIGHT

Chapter Two

THE ROMANS

They called that broken hedge The Haunted Gate.
Strange fires (they said) burnt there at moonless
times.
Evil was there, men never went there late,
The darkness there was quick with threatened
crimes.
And then one digging in that bloodied clay
found, but a foot below, a rotted chest.
Coins of the Romans, tray on rusted tray,
Hurriedly heaped there by a digger pressed.
So that one knew how, centuries before,
some Roman flying from the sack by night,
Digging in terror there to hide his store,
Sweating his pick, by windy lantern light,
Had stamped his anguish on that place's soul,
So that it knew and could rehearse the whole.

John Masefield, *Sonnet LXV*

Some Roman roads which are green lanes have developed hedgerows on one side only.

The compacted agger of this road is formed of flints and small-grade gravel.

Coin hoards such as that mentioned in the poem above are sometimes marked on present-day Ordnance Survey maps. Do such treasures buried in green lanes await the return of a fresh wave of Roman invaders?

In Derbyshire there are hill forts from Mam Tor along the Old Portway, which may have been used by the Romans. Evidence shows that certain sections of Roman roads were once prehistoric tracks; it would be interesting to research into the degree to which Roman roads have been incorporated into our modern-day road system. Many have been kept open and thus have survived well into the twentieth century, but will they continue to do so? Perhaps only if we can learn to appreciate how they were constructed, and to preserve them in some way. An example of such preservation is be found in the case of Watling Street: the Heritage Department of

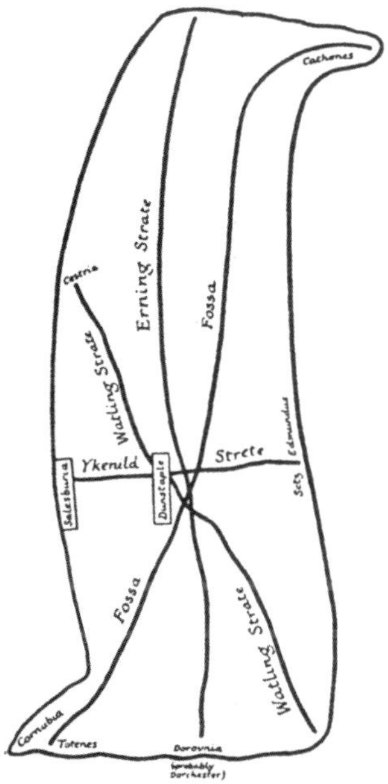

Map circa 1200-1259, showing the four great roads as described by Robert of Gloucester's Chronicle: Watling Street, Ermine Street, the Fosse Way and Icknield Street, now called Icknield Way. (From *Schema Britannica*).

Northamptonshire County Council is in the process of registering the road as an ancient monument (discussed in detail in Chapter Six).

Many books have been written about Roman roads in Britain and how they were constructed; there are maps available for all areas. In the early part of this century, Professor Ivan Margary was the leading light in research on these roads, and an opportunity to study his work on your area could well lead to green lane discoveries.

There is the question of whether or not Roman roads should be included in the category of green lanes at all, as in most cases they were not originally bounded by hedgerows, fences or stone walls. However the drainage channels which existed for causeways up to six or seven feet high means that they were bounded on both sides. In time, within these boundaries, trees and shrubs would take root and form a hedgerow, thus fitting them more comfortably into our definition of green lanes. Roman roads have often been referred to by succeeding generations as 'greenways' or 'green paths'. We must also take into account that many of the

early Ordnance Survey maps show 'Roman roads', the term having been used for many years to describe any routeway of some antiquity. By studying where the major roads ran, their Roman or even earlier origins can be verified.

From Londinium (at London Bridge) the major Roman roads radiated out into their empire. Many years later, Edward the Confessor passed laws to ensure that the principal Roman routes of Watling, Fosse, Hikenild (Icknield) and Ermine were kept clear from sea to sea, as the map opposite shows.

Unfortunately there are many stretches of Roman road which bear the same name. For example there are sections of 'Watling Street' near Hereford, whereas it is meant to pass from Kent through London to Wroxeter. Some sections of these 'long haul' routes still remain green, as do a number of local roads which they reinforced with their system of road-building, but which are not to be principally associated with Roman legions marching throughout the land. Although occupied, the land was also settled and farmed.

When the Romans left, there were those who were ready to follow in their footprints. Lincolnshire County Council have established a Viking Way, which runs for 116 miles (185 km.) from the Humber to Rutland. This

Purple Sunsets

When the legions abandoned this way
to the Iceni once again they left,
in purple sunsets, their regal shadow
now from buzzards not Eagles' wings downflected.

This is the white chalk way
which joins the holloways
of the sunny south-east
to the stark Anglian Plains.

Lands of flat horizons
where fields of woad
were grown to be ground
to powder and painted
purple onto chalk white Ancient Britons
marching over this landscape
reclaiming their ancient road
in the name of a purple God.

Purple sunsets tinged with blood
presaging Viking invasions and fenmen floods.

By the author

contains long stretches of green lane, as does the Icknield Way.

Once the Romans had departed, it was not until 1919 that there was once again a centralized road-building programme in Britain. Our modern motorway map reflects the pattern established by the Romans and prehistoric peoples (see pages 40 & 41). Roads were built by the Romans to give easy access to garrison towns, placed strategically throughout the country; the pattern of our motorway network follows the same principle of ease of access, but has avoided some of their major towns. The equivalent strategy in modern times is to build both new housing developments and hypermarkets close to motorways.

This photograph shows what might not be considered a green lane, but is defined as such in the Guide to the Icknield Way. It is a section of a Roman road cutting through a crop of field rape at Strethall in Essex. RIGHT

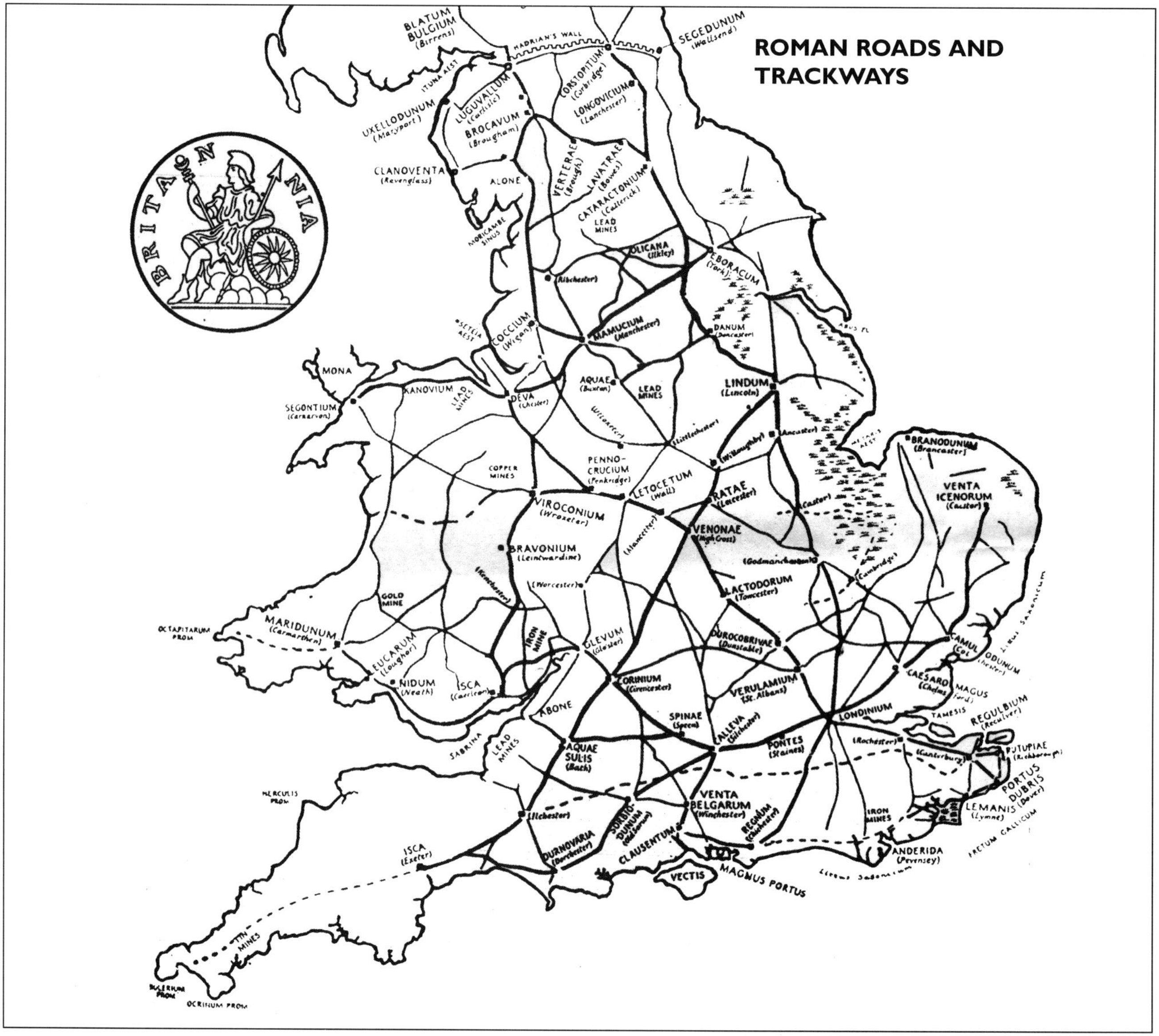
ROMAN ROADS AND TRACKWAYS
BRITANNIA
BLATUM BULGIUM (Birrens)
HADRIAN'S WALL
SEGEDUNUM (Wallsend)
ITUNA AEST
LUGUVALLUM (Carlisle)
CORSTOPITUM (Corbridge)
LONGOVICIUM (Lanchester)
UXELLODUNUM (Maryport)
BROCAVUM (Brougham)
CLANOVENTA (Ravenglass)
ALONE
VERTERAE (Brough)
LAVATRAE (Bowes)
CATARACTONIUM (Catterick)
LEAD MINES
MORICAMBE SINUS
OLICANA (Ilkley)
EBORACUM (York)
(Ribchester)
SETEIA AEST
COCCIUM (Wigan)
MAMUCIUM (Manchester)
DANUM (Doncaster)
ABUS FL
MONA
KANOVIUM
SEGONTIUM (Carnarvon)
DEVA (Chester)
AQUAE (Buxton)
LEAD MINES
LINDUM (Lincoln)
(Uttoxeter)
(Littlechester)
(Willoughby)
(Ancaster)
METARIS AEST
BRANODUNUM (Brancaster)
COPPER MINES
PENNOCRUCIUM (Penkridge)
LETOCETUM (Wall)
RATAE (Leicester)
VIROCONIUM (Wroxeter)
(Castor)
VENTA ICENORUM (Caistor)
BRAVONIUM (Leintwardine)
(Alcester)
VENONAE (High Cross)
(Kenchester)
(Worcester)
(Godmanchester)
(Cambridge)
GOLD MINE
LACTODORUM (Towcester)
OCTAPITARUM PROM
MARIDUNUM (Carmarthen)
IRON MINE
GLEVUM (Gloster)
DUROCOBRIVAE (Dunstable)
CAMULODUNUM (Colchester)
LEUCARUM (Loughor)
NIDUM (Neath)
ISCA (Caerleon)
CORINIUM (Cirencester)
VERULAMIUM (St. Albans)
CAESAROMAGUS (Chelmsford)
ABONE
SPINAE (Speen)
LONDINIUM
TAMESIS
REGULBIUM (Reculver)
SABRINA
LEAD MINES
AQUAE SULIS (Bath)
CALLEVA (Silchester)
PONTES (Staines)
(Rochester)
(Canterbury)
RUTUPIAE (Richborough)
HERCULIS PROM
VENTA BELGARUM (Winchester)
PORTUS DUBRIS (Dover)
(Ilchester)
SORBIODUNUM (Old Sarum)
REGNUM (Chichester)
IRON MINES
LEMANIS (Lymne)
ISCA (Exeter)
DURNOVARIA (Dorchester)
CLAUSENTUM
ANDERIDA (Pevensey)
FRETUM GALLICUM
VECTIS
MAGNUS PORTUS
TIN MINES
BOLERIUM PROM
OCRINUM PROM

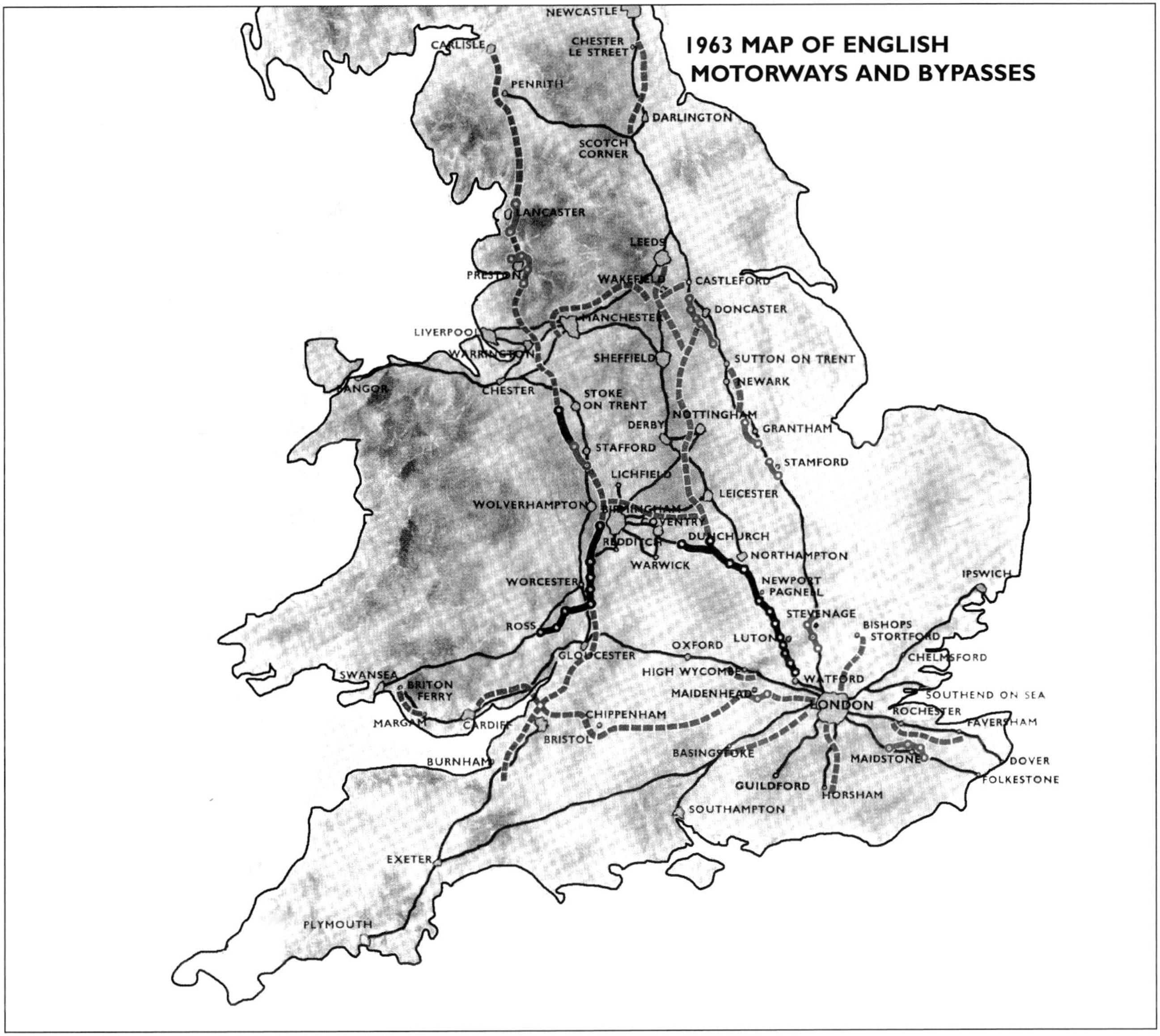
1963 MAP OF ENGLISH MOTORWAYS AND BYPASSES
NEWCASTLE
CARLISLE
CHESTER LE STREET
PENRITH
DARLINGTON
SCOTCH CORNER
LANCASTER
LEEDS
PRESTON
WAKEFIELD
CASTLEFORD
DONCASTER
MANCHESTER
LIVERPOOL
WARRINGTON
SHEFFIELD
SUTTON ON TRENT
NEWARK
BANGOR
CHESTER
STOKE ON TRENT
NOTTINGHAM
DERBY
GRANTHAM
STAFFORD
STAMFORD
LICHFIELD
LEICESTER
WOLVERHAMPTON
DUNCHURCH
NORTHAMPTON
WARWICK
IPSWICH
WORCESTER
NEWPORT PAGNELL
STEVENAGE
ROSS
BISHOPS STORTFORD
LUTON
OXFORD
CHELMSFORD
GLOUCESTER
HIGH WYCOMBE
WATFORD
SWANSEA
BRITON FERRY
MAIDENHEAD
SOUTHEND ON SEA
LONDON
ROCHESTER
CHIPPENHAM
FAVERSHAM
MARGAM
CARDIFF
BRISTOL
BASINGSTOKE
MAIDSTONE
DOVER
BURNHAM
FOLKESTONE
GUILDFORD
HORSHAM
SOUTHAMPTON
EXETER
PLYMOUTH

Chapter Three

BUILDING THE NETWORK

Green Lanes in the Dark Ages

I had not lived in Devon for long. Parked in a lay-by with the old green-covered 2 1/2" map open on the seat, the sound of pounding West Country November rain thudding onto the roof, dripping from the elephant-coloured beech trees, I was lost—lost in the Anglo-Saxon landscape in which we still live today. I readily sympathized with the poet who wrote this some nine hundred years ago:

> Storms break on the hillside,
> the ground bound by driving sleet,
> winter's wrath. Then wanness cometh,
> the night's shade spreadeth, sendeth from north
> the rough hail to harry mankind.
>
> In the earth-realm all is crossed;
> Weird's will changeth the world.
> Wealth is lent us, friendship lent us,
> man is lent, kin is lent;
> all this earth's frame shall stand empty.

From *The Wanderer*, an Anglo-Saxon poem, translated by Michael Alexander.

Because they were green—and vividly so in spring—it may be that these early routeways shone forth for those poor, desperate travellers who crept out onto our highways after the Romans had gone. These travellers would have been the Celts and Ancient Britons, whose main routeways, such as the Icknield Way, had to a certain extent been taken over by the Romans. Having crept out once, they were again about to be sent scurrying back to their villages and valleys by further waves of invaders; and not an environmentally friendly indigenous people's zebra crossing in sight! The great safety—and in some cases sanctity—of the main highway is shown in this quotation from the laws of Kent and Wessex:

> If a man from afar or a foreigner fares through a wood off the highway and neither hollas nor blows a horn, he shall be counted a thief and may be slain or put to ransom.

A green lane at Lydford, an Anglo-Saxon borough established by King Alfred the Great; a number of these Lydford lanes remain green today. The straightness of this lane reflects Anglo-Saxon grid patterns, which can still be seen in some present-day English towns.

LEFT: An Anglo-Saxon lane in Moreleigh, Devon.

Oliver Rackham tells the tale of how one of the earliest 'verge-clearance' laws came into being. It was at Longstowe in Hertfordshire, where a humble carpenter, resident in a highly wooded district, was accused of murdering two wealthy merchants who were passing through from Stamford. In his defence, the accused craftsman said that he was in church.

King Edward I was so shocked by the case that in 1295 he sent out an edict to all the counties of England that all woods through which there was a common right of way should be cut back to a width of sixty feet on either side of the king's road. But before such laws were put in place the Jutes, Anglo-Saxons, Danes and Vikings all came into these lands by sea, and passed along the established highways. It is therefore probably safer to date those green lanes which belong to this period by the dates of invasion rather than of settlement. It has been shown that in many counties the settlements which developed in the Dark Ages had in fact been there in Roman or even pre-Roman times.

So let us take a look at the old prehistoric routes again to see how they were used during this period, and how most of them have remained green until today. The major Roman roads were used to march armies from one administrative centre to another throughout various regions of Britain, whereas the prehistoric routes led to sites of battles and thereafter became associated with official parties travelling throughout the land. Perhaps the main exception to this is the line of Watling Street, which divided the Kingdom of Mercia from Danelaw; parts of this still remain green today.

There are a number of roads which are termed 'harrow' ways and 'herepaths', the word 'here' meaning an invading army (the term appears 221 times in the Anglo-Saxon charters). The Anglo-Saxon chronicle for 875

This mediæval lane, at White Sheet Hill near Shaftesbury, shows evidence of having been widened to accommodate more traffic. Its sunken nature protected travellers from mediæval muggers.

records that the Danes entering from Norfolk got past Cambridge and down to Wareham. They probably came down the Icknield Way and along to the Goring Gap, then to Avebury on the Ridgeway and down to Wareham from Salisbury Plain. They then set up a new fortification point for themselves on a site of an English nunnery between the Frome and Tarrant. They also set up their own fortifications at Wallingford.

The 'herepath' which runs from Shaftesbury over White Sheet Hill to Salisbury may also have formed part of the route of this army.

In Wiltshire there is a 'herepath' leading from Marlborough to Avebury over Fyfield Down, much of which remains green. However 'here' also means grey: there is a Saxon drove road running from Andover to Arlesford, known as Grey Street, which might have been used by a local 'fyrd' (invading army). In association with

Offa's Dyke in Radnor Forest, near Presteign.

these roads to victory we may also find that some 'port ways' have survived as green lanes. These were lanes which led to a town or market, which would often be at a port, and therefore they became known as 'port stræts'. There is one in Derbyshire which runs from Nottingham to Wirksworth and Bakewell. It continues as an ancient trackway running over to Grangemill, here known as the Chariot Way, further evidence that the Romans used routes established by former invaders.

But this was not always the case. At Tamworth in Staffordshire, the Kings of Mercia built their palace in 913 in order to protect their kingdom from the Danes. All their main roads radiated from here, and they ignored the already existing Roman road. These Saxon routes subsequently became most of today's main roads, but one was ignored and remains green today: it runs towards Lichfield over the River Tame.

Some of the lesser military ways may be referred to in old maps as 'cynges ferdstræt', and are worth searching for. That which is known as 'The Cloven Way' in Hampshire, on the outskirts of Melchet Forest, is thought to be the way by which Cerdic and Cynric advanced into Wessex during the late fifth and early sixth centuries.

Another pair of invaders had earlier come to Kent: the famous Hengist and Horsa, who landed in Ebbsfleet in AD 449, Hengist in due course becoming King of Kent. Ebbsfleet was also the landing place of Saint Augustine in AD 597, which makes the lanes in this area rich with historic significance. As is so often the case with estuaryside lanes, they do not fit strictly into the 'with hedgerow' definition of green lanes. However they definitely fall into the GRUTH category, and therefore I am including the lane in the Ebbsfleet area on the Isle of Thanet (TR302585-TR312607), which is known as Green Lane. This is also where the Pilgrim's Way claims great antiquity as being part of the route taken by Cornish tinners carrying their goods to the Continent. It should be remembered that this lane, probably dating

A Saxon boundary bank.

from the first Monastery founded in England (by Augustine on the Isle of Thanet at Minster) has continued to be used for driving sheep from the Ash Levels and Chislet Marshes.

The Chart Hills referred to in the 'Working the Land' section later in this chapter originate in the Norwegian *kartr*, meaning rough, rocky, sterile ground; their position shows how far the Nordic invasions penetrated this vulnerable area of England. Invaders in the north of England came from the coast into the Vale of Pickering, leaving place name evidence in the -ley and -by suffixes to villages and settlements, such as Helmsley, Stokesley and Osmotherley, Ingleby, Easby, Faceby and Swainby. Any lanes or roads in this area could date from these times. One of the best sources for tracing Anglo-Saxon lanes in your area, besides the charters which are explained in more detail in the selected walk (see pages 52 & 53), are Grundy's Ridgeway maps.

A study of Anglo-Saxon charters, with their mention of 'gemære hagan' (boundary hedges), would greatly enrich our knowledge of hedgerows and the evolution of the English landscape; occasionally today we can see where one of these boundary hedges has survived as part of a green lane. The language of the charters was extremely detailed, being based on natural features in the landscape, as is demonstrated by the selected walk. One in six of the features mentioned in these early English charters is to do with highways. Rackham's study of the distribution of terms relating to communications shows that the area in which the highest number of such references appears is the Midlands. This is not surprising, as it was where Celts, Vikings and Saxons would all have crossed at some time.

Following the division of the land into vills (tithings), and prior to the present division into counties, the administrative areas were the Hundreds in the south and the Wapentakes in the north. The Hundred met every four weeks, usually in the open air at a place that was convenient for all members—often at a crossroads. Luckily for today's parish councillors, it was a division of jurisdiction which did not endure. But these Hundred lanes often emerge as some of the most impressive green lanes in England.

> When light begins to glimmer, day to break, on the Dark Ages when daylight begins to flow, wavering, and spreads for us over the Dark Ages, what is the first thing we see? I will tell you what the first thing is that I see, it is the Roads.

So wrote Sir Arthur Quiller Couch, that famous Cornishman who must have been familiar with the Giant's Hedge at West Looe and Lanreath.

Another famous barrier which dates back to these times, and is in part a green lane, is Offa's Dyke. This was constructed in the eighth century by the Saxon King Offa to protect his people from the Welsh and to confirm the boundary of his Mercian Kingdom. The present day route has been constructed around this boundary and runs for 168 miles (270 km.) from the Sedbury Cliffs on the Severn Estuary to Prestatyn in

A boundary bank on 'The Old Hundred Lane' between Bosmere and Hartismere in mid-Suffolk.

North Wales. The original dyke was supposed to be twenty feet high, with a ditch ten feet wide. It is the latter which has turned into a green lane in places, although sometimes it is the hummock of the dyke itself, which is the case as regards the section which passes through Radnor Forest at Presteign.

One of the most spectacular boundary lanes, first identified by Hoskins, is that which divides the Hundreds of Bosmere and Hartismere in mid-Suffolk. Some years ago Hoskins suggested that this lane should be placed under some kind of preservation order. The County Archæologist for Suffolk, whilst agreeing that this should be the case for this 'Old Hundred Lane', said that funds were not available. At present it does not even appear on the register of ancient sites and monuments.

The deep ditches and width of the lane make it unique; it is believed to date from the early tenth century, possibly being the boundary of a large Romano-British estate centred on Stonham Aspal.

In Middlesex there is a large construction known as Grimsdyke, which runs for three miles (5 km.) between Pinner Green and Harrow Weald Common. It is generally believed to have had an agricultural rather than military purpose, but if this is an unploughed headland, the oxen must have been wilder than normal to merit such a barrier being erected to contain them.

The nature of these dykes and ditches has meant that subsidiary lanes have often developed alongside them, in the process creating another form of green lane—associated with the monument, but probably later than it. This has been the case along the Icknield Way (see map in 'The Long Haul' chapter).

In Wiltshire there is a track dating back to a charter of 943, in which its 'hedged way' is referred to, which runs from Witherington Down towards the village of Redlynch (SU208243-204218). Here we see the hedge once again as a boundary and not just as a means of stock-proofing.

In Northamptonshire, part of Watling Street in the Crick area was once an Anglo-Saxon land boundary.

Anglo-Saxon burial sites have been found within the road.

WORKING THE LAND

The progress of deforestation throughout England was one which was already underway by the time this second wave of invaders appeared. The Domesday forests of Melchet, Clarendon, Chute, Savernake and Gravely had all been eaten into, and the invaders carried on the process. The new settlers moved into established centres and worked their way through the wildwood to create new farms and villages. At the time of Domesday (1068) there were only fifty established urban centres, so travel between settlements must have been greater than that between towns. A close look at the pattern of minor roads in any area will show this; they tend to be laid out across the landscape according to topography, and not according to their proximity to the closest town or main road. As Hoskins states:

> If we could have a map of rural Devon in the eleventh century it would look very like the modern O.S. map; practically all the thousands of farm names printed on the modern map would have been on the earlier map, could it have been drawn; and nearly all the thousands of miles of lanes and by-roads would have existed also.

The deforestation referred to above had also been undertaken in the Weald of Kent, the clearings having been used for 'pannage'. This was the ancient right which allowed pigs and cattle to forage in early autumn. The place name elements to look for here are the 'dens' and 'hursts'. Some of the ways which linked them are still green. The Greensand Ridge (the Chart Hills) to the south of Sevenoaks around Toys Hill and Ide Hill provide examples of these. In particular there is one

Bourton Lane, Littlehempston, Devon, showing a dog-leg turn in the lane which indicates where the plough team turned at the head of the field.

called Hogtrough Hill (TQ45873-TQ466557), which provides open views across the Sandstone Ridge.

In many other counties in which deforestation took place around this time one can find green lanes running round the edge of what is now just a remnant of ancient woodland. Such lanes were probably originally woodland rides through the forest. An example can be found at Nun's Lane in Bedfordshire, which now forms part of the Greensand Ridge Walk, and is also a county boundary.

The lane in Littlehempston which cuts through the field (see above) dates from the mediæval period, whereas the 'baulk' or strip of unploughed land at the top centre left of the picture goes back to Anglo-Saxon times.

The diagram on the facing page explains how the system of ploughing led to the adjacent lane formations. Once again, Devon is a good county in which to observe this, the turning plough teams having traced out its small neat fields with bulbous ends.

Other areas of wildwood which were subject to

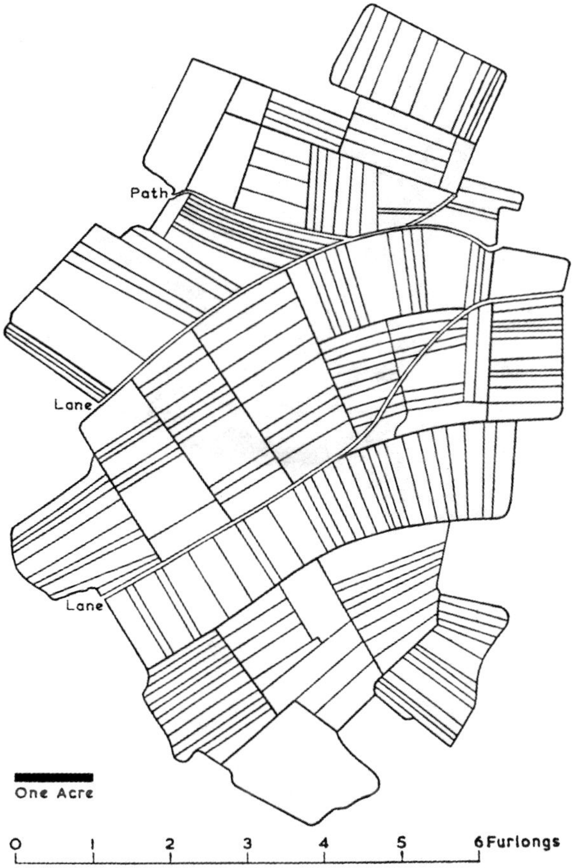

BRAUNTON GREAT FIELD

Fields at Braunton in north Devon, c. 1940, showing Anglo-Saxon field patterns and green lane access routes.

deforestation before and after this period are Rockingham Forest in Northants, Needwood in Staffordshire and Wychwood in Oxfordshire, as well as the Forests of Hainault and Epping in Essex. Within

A green lane showing Anglo-Saxon field patterns in the distance.

these forests you will find place names that reflect the Anglo-Saxon nature of settlement along their lanes.

RELIGIOUS ROUTES

It is during the Dark Ages that Christian Pilgrims are first shown in contemporary pictures, travelling to the various shrines and holy places of their time. Saint Augustine's Chapel was founded in Canterbury in the seventh century, and the monks later moved northward to link up with those of St. Columba in the north. His was a Celtic form of Christianity; some wooden churches remain from this period, notably at Greensted and Jarrow. Viking elements in place names in the north, such as '-by' in Whitby and '-thorpe' in Nunthorpe, are an indication of age. And at Hartlepool Headland there are various lanes with Anglo-Saxon place names associated with the monastery there.

It was in this period that strange Celtic magic was associated with water, and so with wayside wells and fountains. Eight per cent of the places associated with

The lane shown opposite continues, although it is now a private right of way. The Anglo-Saxon runes reflect the shape of the oak trees (see foot of page 53).

Many Anglo-Saxon roads ran through woodland areas: it is worth checking your local woodlands for tracks which have become green lanes.

riverside crossings in Domesday Book became place names. The Anglo-Saxon *brycg* (bridge) sometimes stands for causeway as well.

'Holloway' is a term which is associated with Anglo-Saxon lanes, as well as 'here' and 'harrow'. Although the saltways are dealt with in the 'Pathways for Provisions' chapter, it is worth noting here that the terms 'sealtpath', 'sealstræt' and 'sealtrod' occur eighteen times in Anglo-Saxon charters.

By the end of this period we see roads which came under the King's protection being given a particular definition. They were to be sufficiently wide for two waggons to pass each other, for two oxherds to make their goads touch across them, and for sixteen armed knights to ride side-by-side along them. Henry I strengthened the laws by forbidding any encroachment on these roads, under the heavy penalty of one hundred shillings.

Of course all roads were 'green' during this period, and it was down them that there came one of the swiftest army manœuvres in history. On hearing of William's landing at Pevensey on the south coast in 1066, Harold came down to London from Stamford, where he had just defeated an invading Norwegian Army. It took him just four days to cover the two hundred miles (320 km.), whereas his army took nine.

We now move forward to examine a period when it was not only warriors who were on the move, but the multitudes too.

SEARCHING FOR SAXON PATHS

One of the surest ways of placing a lane in the Anglo-Saxon period is by looking at the Saxon Charters, of which there will be one for your area. The words to look out for are those which contain references to roads, hedges and ditches as boundary markers; these may later have developed into lanes. As Hoskins always championed Devon for its Anglo-Saxon and earlier patterns of settlements, I have chosen a boundary lane to represent

LEFT: Anglo-Saxon charter lane dating back to 962, showing a double boundary bank.

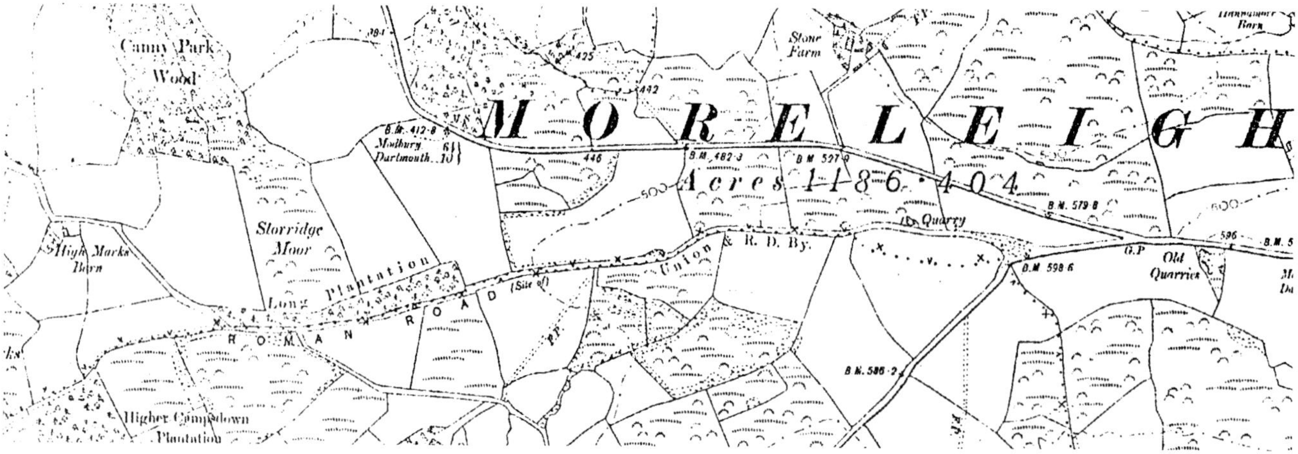

1906 Ordnance Survey map showing Moreleigh Anglo-Saxon lane, referred to here as a Roman road (SX758527-SX739525).

this period—a rather unusual one, as it is for the most part straight and referred to on some maps as a 'Roman Road'. The small field patterns and their distinctive 'ox-turning' shapes are not difficult to recognize in Devon, the Welsh Border counties and Cornwall; they contribute to the uniqueness of their landscape.

Weighing up the evidence given by the counties that responded to my questionnaire when making this study, it would seem that it is the boundary lane which best represents Saxon days. In King Edgar's charter of 962, an area of land is marked out from Kingsbridge up to Moreleigh, containing between nine and ten thousand acres of land. The parish of Moreleigh (meaning 'watery clearing in a forest'), where the lane is to be found, stands relatively high in Devonshire's South Hams area and has clear views out to Dartmoor. At the beginning of the lane, there is a view of the moor, which seems to be very close, its sweeping lines taking up all the horizon. From here you can look out over the small field patterns which are so characteristic of this Saxon-settled land. You will then enter the tree-lined lane: there are elders, sallow, blackthorn, hawthorn, oak and ash. The Saxon runes for the latter reflect the shape of the tree silhouettes; the dipping branches of the ash Æsc and the rising, spreading branches of the oak Ac. Past the pines, the double hedgebank on the right of the lane becomes very apparent. As well as being the charter boundary, this is also the parish boundary marker, recognizable by the double rows of trees—one in the lane and one on the outer bank. Just beyond where the tarmac remnants of the surface break up there is a beautiful group of beech trees growing from a moss-covered bank. Behind these trees, before the conifer copse begins, is a patch of waste: a reminder that in the Domesday Book of 1086 'underwood' was often recorded. Suddenly we are at the end of the green lane section of the charter boundary. Going on a little further, you will see a gate on the bend to your left.

Through here is a double line of oaks on private land, no doubt a continuation of this boundary and of this lane, which once ran all the way down through woodland to the River Avon.

The tarmacked lane which still follows the line of the charter is very different from the section of lane which

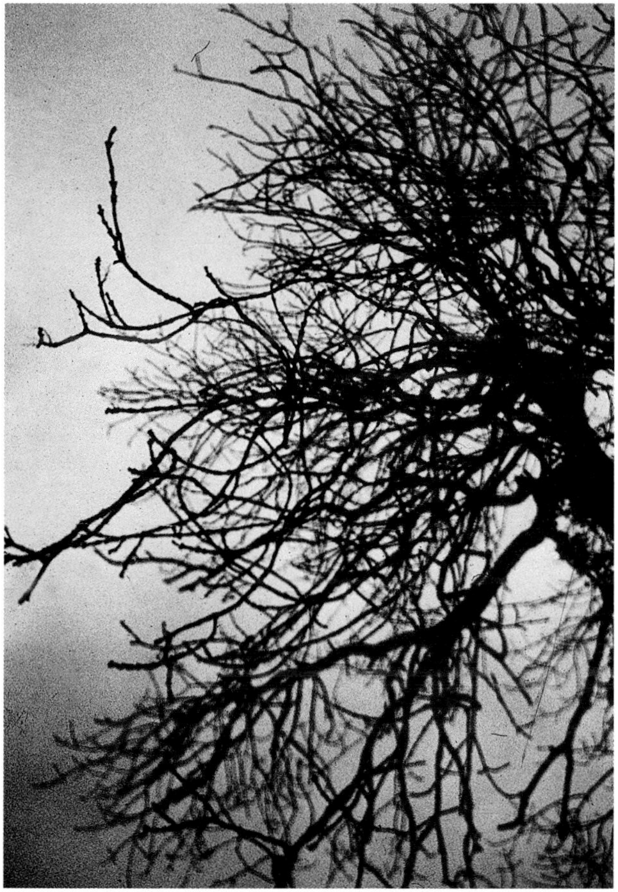

Ash tree, used in Anglo-Saxon symbolism.

ᚫ Ash rune (Æsc tree)

ᚪ Oak rune (Ac tree)

you have just walked through, even though they are of the same age. In the Moreleigh Mount section alone, even on the brightest day, you will feel the age of this lane—although (if in company) you may fall into talking of other things and forget the lane. It has been trodden for over a thousand years and remains unworn, a fine example of the magic of green lanes.

Follow the lane down to Gara Bridge, the 'wealdenes ford' of the charter (the bridge itself incorporating an Anglo-Saxon place name) and return via the winding road up to Moreleigh Mount again.

Lanes which date from this period are rarely signposted. But, as the historian Hoskins says, "Every lane has its history: it is not there by accident, and every twist it makes once had some historical meaning which we can decipher today, but not often." These Anglo-Saxon lanes chart the agricultural settlement of the countryside, although today's agricultural patterns are completely different. There are probably more short stretches of green lanes dating back to Saxon times than to any other: in urban areas they may survive as Unadopted Roads. I would urge you and your community to adopt them! If they are not long enough for walking the dog, then they may be useful as short cuts for foxes and badgers. In any event, their wildlife value is immense.

The other type of Saxon lane which needs preserving is the Anglo-Saxon boundary and charter lane, many of which have disappeared with field enlargement schemes. But with the new 'set aside' and countryside stewardship schemes, wildlife sanctuaries are created along field edges where such boundaries run. So whether you are adopting an urban Saxon orphan or protecting a charter boundary lane, you will be preserving our Saxon heritage of green lanes.

Chapter Four

MEETING THE MARKETS

Green Lanes in the Mediæval & Elizabethan Periods

> There are, as I take it, few great townes in England that have not their weeklie markets, one or more granted from the prince, in which all manner of provision for the house-hold is to be bought and sold, for ease and benefit of the countrie round about.
>
> Harrison, *Of Faires and Markets 1577-87*

The nature of roads in mediæval England was very much dependent on this emerging pattern of markets and fairs, to which an increasingly mobile local population demanded access. Many green lanes which are still with us today date from these times, and trade was the driving force in this growing communication network. Markets were established by royal charter: a look at any map which shows the early development of an area will reveal a sudden proliferation in the thirteenth and fourteenth centuries. But some were more successful than others, as is demonstrated by the remains of a fair and market to be found by the holloway at Burgate Hall in mid-Suffolk.

Tracks which had existed from prehistoric and Roman times, and had been consolidated by the settlements made in the dark ages, were sometimes incorporated in the ways to these new markets. The holloways which belong to this period are sometimes, surprisingly, more sunken than lanes of an earlier date, because they were short cuts between settlements, as opposed to planned routes such as the ridgeways and causeways of the 'Long Haul' chapter.

In 1285 the Statute of Winchester was passed, putting the responsibility for the maintenance of highways firmly on the shoulders of the Lords of the Manor. If a road became impassable, it was permitted to form another, running parallel to it. Prior to this, one of the three responsibilities which landowners owed the monarch was to pay for the upkeep of roads and bridges, the other two being to contribute to the armed forces and to fortifications. This was a poll tax paid by the wealthy, which both kept them safe and enabled them to move about the countryside which they owned and ruled.

Many market towns were situated on main roads to catch the passing trade. At Higham Ferrers in Northamptonshire, the Earl of Derby created a Borough in 1251, giving instant burgher status to ninety villagers of Higham.

Other examples can be found at Bewtry in Nottinghamshire, New Malton in Yorkshire, Henley-in-Arden in Warwickshire, Pontefract in Yorkshire, Dunstable in Bedfordshire and Baldock in Herts. A detailed study of the markets and fairs associated with these towns is likely to show a network of green lanes which once led to the sites where they were held. Sometimes roads were diverted to bring traffic into a town, such as at Appleby in Westmoreland and St. Ives in Huntingdonshire, where the old crossing by the ford at Slepe was replaced by a new bridge.

But there were other reasons for travel. The monarchs

LEFT: A mediæval lane leading to woodlands, which once covered a much greater area of the countryside than they do today.

Mediæval cortège entering a city. The itineraries of monarchs such as Edward I often show routes which have now become green lanes.

John and Edward I liked to keep in touch with their subjects, and there exist detailed itineraries which trace their journeys through England at the time. Inevitably, some of the places which were important then are not so today; green lanes may be discovered by following one such route carefully.

An example of such an itinerary—a particularly famous one—is the route taken by the coffin of Queen Eleanor of Castille on its final journey (she was married to Edward I, the great traveller king mentioned above). The overnight resting places are the sites of the twelve Eleanor Crosses, of which only three survive. The route began in Hadby near Lincoln, then proceeded to Grantham, Stamford, Geddington, Northampton, Stony Stratford, Woburn, Dunstable, St. Albans, Waltham Cross, West Cheap and finally Charing Cross.

The most famous of these resting places for the coffin was Charing Cross. Today this monument stands sadly neglected outside the station, with no indication as to its poignant origin and historical significance. (And close to Geddington, motorway drivers may question the appropriateness of the name of the Queen Eleanor interchange.) One can imagine how difficult it must have been to make this journey, which Taylor retraces in his book *Roads and Tracks of Britain*. Of all the ways which are being rediscovered and made into National Trails, this might be a good one to restore. In the process, the various monuments upon the way could receive some funding to be suitably refurbished where required.

There are other less exotic corpse ways (also known as 'lichways' or 'lychways') throughout the country. These date back to the time when parishes were very large, and are usually found in areas of moorland, heath and wasteland. When a parishioner died, his or her body would be transported to the parish church, which could be as far as forty miles (65 km.) away. There could be other reasons for this journey: on Dartmoor, all those who died within the forest boundaries had to be buried at Lydford; coming from Widecombe-on-the-Moor, for example, would involve you in a long trek. Part of the way at Baggator is along enclosures which form a kind of lane known as a 'stroll'.

On a more humble level, there were the Bishop's

Visitations throughout his parishes. A map from Staverton in Devon shows just where Bishop Stapleton went on his Visitations over the years between 1281 and 1341. Some of these places were reached by green lanes which still exist today. Then there are the pilgrims' routes of this period to Canterbury, Walsingham and further afield to Santiago de Compostela in Spain. This last destination provides what may be the quirkiest evidence of mediæval green lanes. In order to get to Spain, the pilgrims first had to find a suitable embarkation point. One of the most atmospheric is at Landulph in Cornwall: a group of lanes lead from Paradise Lane to a landing quay where, in 1434, 160 pilgrims were granted licences to seek out the shrine of St. James at Santiago.

A reaper's cart going uphill. From the 14th century Louterell Psalter.

The practice of travelling to visit chantry chapels or local saints' shrines also belongs to this period, and some wayside crosses mark the routes of these journeys. In Cornwall there are a series of Saints Ways which have such crosses, some of which are sited on green lanes. One of the most famous routes upon which people travelled for religious purposes was the Pilgrim's Way, which ran from Winchester via London to the shrine of St. Thomas à Becket in Canterbury.

In the sixteenth century, Henry VIII had the shrine destroyed. Pilgrimages ceased, but the route, approximately 120 miles (200 km.) long, is still traceable today and many sections have the character of a green lane.

A secular reason for travelling was to the Appleby Horse Fair in Cumbria, which has several green lanes leading to it. The fair is said to have its origins in the thirteenth century, although James II was the first to issue a charter for "the purchase of and sale of all manner of goods, cattle, horses, mares, and geldings" in 1685. The fair still takes place annually in June.

In the Peak district, there is the Mediæval Way from Leek to Macclesfield, on which at Cleulow a cross stands by a mediæval holloway; many other examples of religious ways marked by crosses can be found. In Sampford Courtenay in Devon, all the green lanes which lead out of the village are marked with a cross. These crosses may have been put up in the aftermath of the Prayer Book massacre which took place by the church in 1549, with the aim of warding off any further evil intent towards the village's inhabitants.

Line of mediæval road through Bulwick Park.

Mediæval wayside cross.

In a more peaceful vein, there are the various ways which connected monasteries to other religious establishments within their jurisdiction. These are known as cartulary or chartulary routes, their principal use being for the safe carrying of mediæval documents and charts by the precursors of modern-day couriers. There are also a number of church paths which remain as green lanes; it is believed that these were primarily used for Rogation and other religious ceremonies based around the Church. There is a holloway north of the church at Higham in Suffolk which dates from this period.

The mediæval period also saw the beginnings of 'Perambulations'. Charters were issued which gave landowners the right to set boundaries as a safeguard against deforestation by others. The first such Perambulation on Dartmoor was made in 1240. The places where these boundaries were drawn can often be the origins of green lanes.

MEDIÆVAL TRAVELLING

Chaucer's *Canterbury Tales* gives us a full and vivid account of the variety of travellers in mediæval times. In many ways it has never been bettered as the ultimate road novel: just consider the variety of characters he portrays. There are the clerics of varying degrees of piety, the lawyers, the merchants and the military men—not to mention the Wife of Bath.

Although we have seen that the Statute of Winchester gave powers to the lords of the manor to maintain the roads, at this time there were also 'way-wardens' who were appointed under Common Law to supervise voluntary labour on the roads.

The other main sources of information about the history of lanes in mediæval times are the Court Manorial Rolls, which give details of court cases concerned with highway maintenance:

> Richard Pynnwyll submitted to the judgement of the court on the charge of allowing his pigs to wander at large on the Queen's Highway and was fined 3s. 4d. Stoke [*Stokenham*] nr. Kingsbridge in Devon. (1562)

Road transport continued to be more expensive than water transport throughout this period and into

Many green lanes date from the foundation of church walks, which were much used in mediæval times. RIGHT

These illustrations from the Ellesmere manuscript show Chaucer's pilgrims: the Wife of Bath, the Lady Prioress and the Cook.

Elizabethan and Stuart times. It cost 1s 3d per ton-mile for the transport of goods which were fragile or perishable. The cost of transporting oak timber a distance of fifty miles (80 km.) was equivalent to the cost of the timber itself. So what prompted this special delivery, which is to be found recorded in 1309?

> A big consignment of timber from Gamlingay to Grantchester at Christmas in hard frost.

Was it for the repair of the mill, or for the immediate construction of the Grantchester dam, despite the imminence of the Christmas festivities? This is an example of guesswork based on the documentary evidence that we have, but it can sometimes lead to asking the right questions that are needed to provide a more accurate picture of a road's history.

The rate at which people travelled overland varied according to the method of transport and the purpose of their travels. Walking on foot at approximately 2-4 miles per hour, one would cover 15 to 25 miles in a day; running at 6-7 m.p.h., one would cover 30 to 40 miles; and a horse moving at 12-15 m.p.h. would also cover 30 to 40 miles, allowing for rest breaks. When making a day trip to market, it was not considered practical to travel more than 20 miles (32 km.) in all, as besides the journey itself there was the business of buying and selling. Being tired, having made a bad deal, or awaiting payment for goods—any of these reasons could lead to a dealer or merchant considering taking over a 'purpresture' on the way back from market. Purprestures, often also referred to as squatters' cottages, can sometimes be found on a green lane, when a dwelling suddenly appears in the middle of its length.

It was certainly a dangerous period in which to be travelling. Some Lords of the Manor employed gangs of robbers to patrol the highways on their land and rob passers-by. When the felons were brought to justice in front of the Lord of the Manor, they were invariably found innocent or given small tasks to perform, for which the Lord would be duty-bound to offer payment.

Weapons were the privilege of the rich, so most travellers made do with what were known as quarterstaves, the poles which feature in the battles between Friar Tuck and Little John. They were twirled above the travellers' heads, making a roaring noise in order to warn any robbers lurking nearby that the travellers were armed, albeit in this primitive fashion.

By Norman times there had come into being a popular standard for the width of roads which fell under the King's protection, as described on page 51.

An example of the implementation of Edward I's Trench Act (see Chapter One) in an ancient woodland can be found in the parish of Long Melford in Suffolk: Lineage Wood, about ninety acres in all, which dates back to 1386. A track running from east to west, with a wood bank on the north side, marks the edge of the original wood. There is also a length of holloway at TL88654821.

Although we are still primarily in an age of sledges and packhorses, carriages and carts are beginning to be used, which must have been detrimental to the conditions of the lanes—especially in winter. I had a conversation with a retired Devon farmer who remembers taking flour to the local mill by waggon. He often had to stop and unload the waggon; place down 'bavines' (bundles of twigs) on the track to make it firm; take the horses and waggon across, and then load the waggon up again with the flour, doing this several times during his journey. No doubt this was a mediæval practice too. Sometimes records reveal a heartening upturn in the history of a lane: in Raunds in Northamptonshire, a lane known as Midland Road in 1407 became known as Hardgravel Lane in 1458, which shows that some upgrading had been done.

However, most roads deteriorated during the Elizabethan period, owing to the methods of maintenance. Following on from the Acts already mentioned, with the passing of the 1555 Highway Act the Church was no longer responsible for the maintenance of roads. This Act of Parliament put the responsibility onto the local parish, through the form of 'voluntary' enforced labour. For four days out of every year (subsequently increased to six), you would toil on the roads; an unpaid surveyor was appointed to allot the work. It is interesting to note that where records of work done under this system survive, the lanes best repaired are those close to the surveyor's holdings! You were fined if you refused the office of surveyor, or refused to work.

This new Act brought about some improvements to

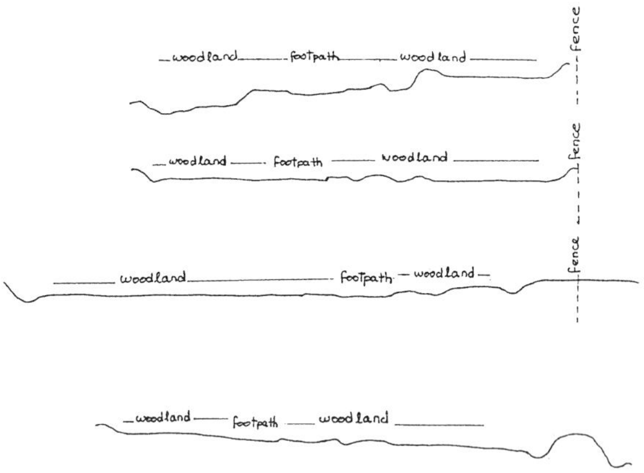

Measurements along the Hog's Back Trackway, taken from the centre of the bank on the Loseley side (south) to the centre of the bank on the Guildford Park side (north), using the bank on the south side as a base line.

the state of the roads, but there was a lack of funds for purchasing the necessary materials. The workers were soon known as:

> the King's loiterers, who work when they list, come and go at their pleasure, and spend most of their time standing still and prating.

BRIDGE-BUILDING

For a large part of this period, bridge-building remained the prerogative of the church, as is indicated by the ecclesiastically pointed arches of early bridges. First let us consider those of a single arch construction. These were constructed where rivers were liable to high spate; we see a lot of them in Cumbria, Northumberland and Derbyshire. They are also to be found at watersheds on the edge of moors such as Exmoor and Dartmoor.

The common occurrence of people falling off these bridges, or being swept away in floods, is recorded throughout history. One who did not take such a chance was Thomas Ferris, a poor boy who was courting one Agnes Richardson who lived on the other side of Egton Bridge on the river Esk in Cumbria. In order to advance his status, and so gain the hand of the woman he loved, he decided to go to sea. On the night of his leaving from Whitby, he went to bid farewell to Agnes. Unfortunately the river was in full spate, which prevented him from crossing. Agnes remained faithful; he became rich and eventually achieved the position of Mayor of Hull. In 1619 he built Beggar's Bridge, to prevent other couples from being thus parted.

Packhorse bridges at Littlehempston, Devon.

Staverton Bridge in south Devon has a similar, but more tragic, tale to tell: how a bridge and groom were swept away on their wedding day by the floods coming over the parapets.

Ambushes frequently occurred at bridges, as they were an unavoidable part of a journey. Staverton Bridge, when it was built of wood, saw at least two violent incidents, one of which went to court. In 1436 a curate was attacked by a man and his wife; he turned upon his attacker and killed him. On his deathbed the attacker confessed his crime and was forgiven by the Bishop. However there were other ways of obtaining forgiveness, which could be in the form of an indulgence. These were given to those who had committed crimes but were prepared to work on bridge construction or repairs. In 1457 there was a brawl on Staverton Bridge, during which the Bailiff of the Haytor Hundred was attacked and robbed. His men retaliated by taking back the stolen goods, but a dagger was drawn—a criminal offence. To atone for this, this early form of community service seems appropriate.

The original site of a bridge can often be precisely located by the roads and the hedges which flanked them. Consider this part of a description of the Small Bridge in Totnes:

> ...in the South of lands of Barnard Smyth called the Priors Marsh and the North hedge of the said close 8 land yards and in breadth from the West hedge adjacent the Small bridge unto the East hedge...

There were chantry chapels on some bridges; the most famous of these are now tarmacked. However St. Ives Bridge in Huntingdonshire is now closed to vehicular traffic of all kinds, so it may become green once again.

Haft of cross used as parapet for mediæval bridge.

The tolls collected on such bridges normally went towards the upkeep of the chapels, but if there was no chapel the money was used for another purpose, such as the maintenance of a teacher in a free grammar school.

As we are now entering the age of map-making, where fords, stepping stones and other crossing places feature, from this time onwards we can date the green lanes leading to them with some accuracy.

MEDIÆVAL LANES AND AGRICULTURE

Before going on to consider examples of mediæval lanes in various counties, let us look at the form of mediæval villages and fields. The mediæval system of strip farming gave three forms of access; all of which can still be identified today in the form of green lanes.

1. *Unfenced trackways* which occur in Buckinghamshire, Warwickshire, Northamptonshire and Leicestershire. They run along the headland of the fields, giving access for the coming and going of the oxen that ploughed the field and the subsequent gathering of crops. In Cheshire, from Shocklach to Wetreins Green and beyond, there is a byway which shows evidence of a mediæval ridge and furrow at its beginning at Castleton (for further details see Chapter Six).

2. *Assart lands*, mentioned earlier when we looked at the deforestation of land in Saxon times; some lanes which lead to these sites are still green today. In the Midlands they are to be found in Sherwood, Needwood, Wychwood and Rockingham; also in the Weald of Kent and in Epping and Hainault Forests in Essex.

3. *Unenclosed waste or moorland* in the north of England and *heathlands* in the south: where lanes formerly led into these areas, dramatic forms of mediæval road can sometimes be found. The Earls Way in Derbyshire, dating from 1200, leads from Caldon Grange near Ashbourne (GR086486) to Earlsway House in Staffordshire (GR914618).

There are some anomalies to these agricultural patterns, such as those roads in Kent which, dating back to pre-mediæval droving days, must be mediæval or older. Some of the more unusual ones can be found by the coastal area at the southern end of Romney Marsh known as Walland Marsh (meaning 'stranger').

Some green lanes provide evidence of access paths

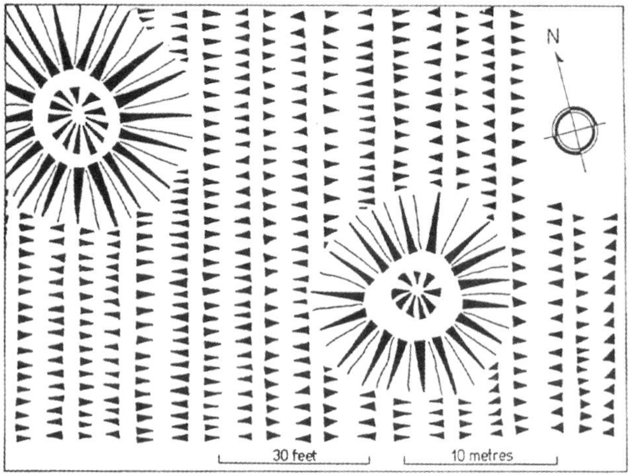

A 12th-century map from Yorkshire showing ridge and furrow patterns of agriculture. Green lanes provided access to this system.

Photograph from St. Martins in the Isles of Scilly, showing small fields with an access green lane.

used by warreners to tend the breeding grounds of rabbits, which were first recorded in England in the twelfth century but extensively farmed from mediæval times onwards.

DESERTED VILLAGES

Names that promise the most evocative kind of green lanes seldom live up to expectation. Where a village has been deserted, the lane that leads to it will also disappear in time. This is confirmation of the theory, as expounded at the beginning of this book, that green lanes only continue to exist as long as they are used.

History is nothing if not contradictory, so I now quote from Christopher Taylor (author of *The Roads and Tracks of England*), who points out that the Curia Regis rolls for 1241 show a right of way from a place called Philipston in Dorset towards a wood called Suthden. Today it seems that the right of way still exists, despite the village having disappeared. Although some of these vanishing villages were the result of the Black Death (1348-9), there were other factors which came into play, both before and after this date, which led to the desertion of villages.

The Black Death can be used as a convenient time from which to date some small fields in the Midlands. As more and more land was taken for grazing and less and less for arable, especially in the Midlands, we see the beginnings of enclosures long before the Great Enclosure Acts of the eighteenth century. The following rhyme was written by a drover reporting on economic matters in Elizabethan times.

More plenty of mutton and beef,
Corn, butter and cheese of the best,
More wealth anywhere (to be brief)
More people, more handsome prest,
Where find ye (go search any coast)
Than there where enclosures are most.

A mediæval plough.

Many families were evicted to make way for the grazing of sheep for wool, so some of these deserted villages are the consequence of a cold-hearted policy towards the workers upon whom the landowners had once relied. The contemporary mapmaker John Norden was appalled by such behaviour, writing:

> When the ox and sheep shall feed where good houses stood... who wil not say it is the bane of a commonwealth, an apparent badge of Atheism and an argument of waspish ambition or wolvish emulation.

Maurice Beresford's book *History on the Ground* records many examples of such behaviour, particularly at Fawsley in Northamptonshire.

Some green lanes which date from mediæval times once led to manor houses or castles; some are still standing, and some lie in ruins. The English (and Americans) will always go along to visit a ruin, however nugatory: there is something about a half-standing wall which draws their attention. In Hereford there are the ruins of Aberedw: this is Marcher country where the Norman lords tried to keep the wild Welsh at bay by building castles and fortifications along the borders. This castle, now completely razed to the ground, is at the end of a lane (currently used for parking industrial plant) which was once the final refuge of the last Prince of independent Wales. Llewelyn ap Gruffyd became separated from his army as a result of treachery and took refuge there; he escaped from his pursuers, but was killed near Builth Wells. Also along the border is Goodrich Castle, built to defend the crossing of the Wye. There are a lot of green lanes and tracks round the castle which have now been closed to the public.

On the Suffolk coast at Otley there are several mediæval house platforms and holloways in a three-acre meadow.

Then there are the small local quarries from which stone was taken to build manor houses. If you find a hilltop which has trees growing at an unexpectedly horizontal angle, look for a hollow below and you may find a track which leads from here in the direction of the great house nearby (although the great house itself, of course, may have gone).

In Staffordshire, between Elford and Wigginton (SK206090), there is a network of lanes which dates from the eighteenth century enclosures. Between these wide field divisions, typical of the Great Enclosures, a lane remains which connects the deserted mediæval village site at Syerscote with another known as Old Almington—the word 'old' being proof enough. Similarly in Bedfordshire there is a group of lanes round Totternhoe which seems to link the villages in the area together.

The economic collapse which led to the desertion of villages can sometimes be connected to the development of roads which drew traffic away from them. Today, in a strange reversal of this process, many villages are being spoiled because they are so accessible via the main road network. From these main roads come visiting cars which need to be parked; if there is a disused lane to hand, it will quickly be blocked as a result of impromptu car parking.

Local markets of all kinds must be good for the local

economy. If we can obtain what we need locally, we will not need to use our cars to travel great distances in pursuit of our provisions. However a type of market which has recently sprung up in the same way as the mediæval markets did is the 'car boot sale'. Unlike its mediæval counterparts, many car boot sales are held specifically on the one holy day of the week that we technically still have—on Sundays, when all good cars deserve a rest.

One can imagine that in mediæval times there were farmers who rejoiced at finding that a few of their fields would bring in revenue from a weekly market; and that there were other farmers who fumed at the loss of land for farming purposes. Similarly, today there are arguments for and against the regularization and legalization of car boot sales. They can give new life to a green lane—or destroy it.

Mediæval lane showing evidence of packhorse ledges (see Chapter Six for further details).

The Queen's Highway, now a green lane and a public footpath, at East Allington in Devon. RIGHT

Hellond medow.
Ley hills
South
Norris his clo
Myll tongue
The Queenes
Mill forde.
The way to the myll.
Myll medow.
West
house

Chapter Five

A GREEN THOUGHT IN A GREEN SHADE

The Ecological Value of Green Lanes

Annihilating all that's made
into a green thought in a green shade.
Andrew Marvell, *The Garden*

This chapter deals with green lanes as havens for wildlife, a subject dear to the hearts of many environmentalists. Unexpectedly, it has turned out to be the shortest chapter: this is because there are now many books—already in print or in gestation—which cover in great detail the subject of hedgerows and their importance in the landscape. Here we will look at the elements which make up a green lane, as defined in the first chapter, from an ecological point of view.

The foliage along such lanes is nearly always green, whatever the time of year. There is a poem by Edward Thomas about lanes in Essex, which sums up the feeling of how important they are botanically and otherwise, no matter what the season.

THE LANE
Some day, I think, there will be people enough
In Froxfield to pick all the blackberries
Out of the hedges of Green Lane, the straight
Broad lane where now September hides herself
In bracken and blackberry, harebell and dwarf gorse.
To-day, where yesterdays a hundred sheep
Were nibbling, halcyon bells shake to the sway
Of waters that no vessel ever sailed...
It is a kind of spring: the chaffinch tries
His song. For heat it is like summer too.
This might be winter's quiet. While the glint
Of hollies dark in the swollen hedges lasts—
One mile—and those bells ring, little I know
Or heed if time be still the same, until
The lane ends and once more all is the same.

THE NATURAL HEDGEROW

Many wildlife trusts and natural history societies have made surveys to record the value of their hedgerow lanes. The form in Appendix I at the back of the book will give you some idea of how to go about making a survey of your own.

At the foot of the form there is a reference to hedge-dating. The essence of this theory is that by counting the different number of species of trees along one side of a thirty-yard stretch of hedge we can tell how old the hedge is: each species is taken to represent a hundred years. The best way to test the theory is by reference to historical evidence such as a charter, records of perambulations or the beating of a parish boundary. (For a fuller appreciation of hedge-dating theory refer to Pollard and Hooper's book on *The Hedge* in the Collins' Naturalist series. There is also a very good account of hedgerow trees in Oliver Rackham's *History of the Countryside*.) The illustrations on the next two pages give some idea of the variety of trees which co-exist in a hedge.

A hedge which consists of one species only is most

LEFT: Ash hedge in a lane.

COMMON PLANTS TO BE FOUND IN GREEN LANES

A cross-section of a typical sunken green lane, showing some of the plants found and their approximate locations. Note that this list is by no means exhaustive, and the species listed do not represent the flora found in a single green lane.

Purple Vetch

Comfrey

Ivy-leaved Toadflax

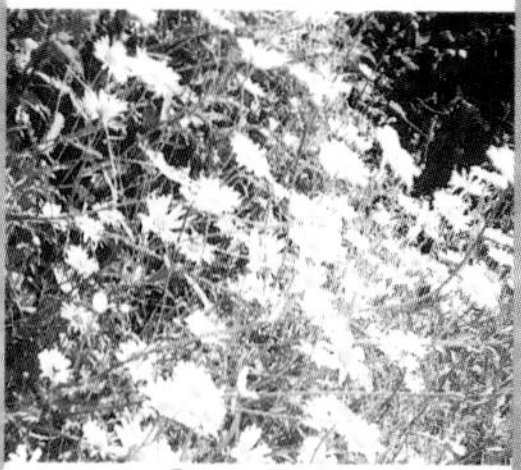
Oxeye Daisy

Fumitory

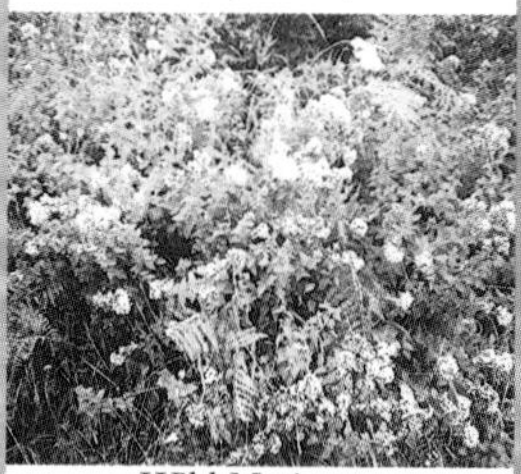
Wild Marjoram

Buckler Fern

Rosebay Willowherb

Pencilled Crane's-bill

Sheep's Sorrell

Bluebell
Bramble
Black Bryony
Cleavers
Common Fumitory
Dog's Mercury
Hedge Bedstraw
Common Cow-wheat
Creeping Cinquefoil
Foxglove
Hard Fern
Hart's-tongue Fern
Hedge Woundwort
Herb-Robert
Maidenhair Spleenwort
Nettle

Black Medick

Arum
Bird's-foot-trefoil
Black Medick
Bush Vetch
Clover
Common Vetch

Cow Parsley
Cut-leaved Crane's-bill
Goats-beard
Green Alkanet
Ground Ivy

Red Valerian

Bluebell

Mugwort

Male Fern

Pennywort
Pignut
Polypody
Poppy
Purple Vetch
Red Campion
Soft Shield Fern
Spotted Medick
Three-Cornered Leek
Violets
White Dead-nettle
Wild Strawberry
Willowherb
Wood-rush
Yellow Archangel

Maidenhair Spleenwort

Knapweed

Polpody

Tormentil

Hairy Tare
Herb-bennet
Hogweed
Lady's Bedstraw
Lesser Trefoil
Meadow Vetchling

Pine Apple Mayweed
Silverweed
Speedwell
Stitchwort
Tufted Vetch
Yarrow

Green Alkanet

Barren Strawberry

Common Chickweed

Illustrations by Steve Taylor

likely to belong to the Enclosure period of hedge planting in the eighteenth century. Certain areas of England are home to particular species of trees: in Essex, for example, hedges used to be comprised chiefly of elm (now coming back after the ravages of Dutch Elm Disease), mixed with dogwood, maple and spindle. One of the fascinations of making a habit of hedge-dating wherever you may be is that strange anomalies sometimes present themselves. Garden escapees such as lilac, buddleia and privet have invaded ancient hedgerows all over the country. Many of the green lanes in the Scilly Isles are bordered by escalonia.

The presence of very large trees in a hedge could be evidence of a labourer's insurance policy. At the turn of the century, a labourer starting work in a farm where he knew he was likely to spend the rest of his life would choose a sapling growing in a hedgerow at the beginning of his career and earmark it so that he could claim it at the end of his working life, as a retirement bonus. These large trees also stood as markers for travellers. 'Hedgebot' was the term given to the 'fruits of the hedge' which could be collected legally by labourers, supplying them with firewood, tool handles, thatching spars and, where appropriate, willow for weaving.

Today, large trees left in a lane are extremely valuable for the wildlife which they harbour, including owls and other birds of prey. Insects in the fissures of large broadleaved trees such as oaks and chestnuts are food for woodpeckers and tree creepers.

In the first chapter we looked at the various habitats through which green lanes pass. I live in Devon, so it is natural that this book will have a certain regional bias; but it is also undeniable that Devonshire hedges are particular rich in wildlife. In 1976 Robin Ravilious won the Kenneth Allsop Memorial Prize with an essay on her 'ordinary' hedge in North Devon. Here is an extract:

> On regular hedgerow inspections I began a list of its flora and fauna. The trees would furnish a handsome wood: oak, ash, elm, hawthorn, blackthorn, buckthorn, holly, elder, spindle, wild cherry and hazel. All of them were once useful timber to trades and crafts ranging from shipbuilding to the making of lace bobbins. If nothing else they made faggots, in some districts the poor man's only firewood. Alas, our hedge is put to few such uses now, beyond supplying our thatcher with home-grown spars.
>
> In autumn it is a poor man's orchard. Wild raspberries exquisitely flavoured are followed by rose-hips for syrup, elderberries for exotic jelly, blackberries, nuts, crab apples and finally sloes for sloe gin. The flowers' list numbers twenty-nine, though there may well be more. It begins with the snowdrops which thread a white ribbon almost at eye level along the top of the bank. Later, a stream of bluebells takes their place, then dog's mercury and campion. On the southern side are stitchwort, foxglove, gorse and broom, and the handsome pink mallow beneath a cascade of dog-rose and honeysuckle. Behind them is a carpet of obscurer herbs, gradually identified: ground ivy, wood sage, herb-bennet and bedstraw, many of which must once have found their way into our cottage for herbal remedies.

To linger a little longer on the Devonshire hedge, there is this description given in the eighteenth century:

> HEDGEROWS. The Danmonian Fence is common to the South Hams. High Mounds surmounted by coppice wood. Not a hedgerow Tree, nor a Pollard is seen, in a hundred square miles! As naked of Hedge Timber, as the recently inclosed lands of Leicestershire. Perhaps

COMMON HEDGEROW TREES AND SHRUBS TO BE FOUND IN GREEN LANES

Holly

Common Dog Rose

Elder

Honeysuckle

Other likely species besides those illustrated:

Ash
Beech
Blackthorn
Briar
Dogwood
Elm
Elder
Hawthorn
Sycamore
Sweet Chestnut
Wych Elm

Hazel hedgerow

Oak

Blackthorn blossom

Blackthorn sloes

the sea air is an enemy to Hedgerow Trees. Or the high mounds of this Country are not fit to receive them. Or the life-lease tenure has an interest in preventing their rising.

Throughout England you will find green lanes rich in hardwood species of hedgerow trees. They are home to over forty varieties of birds and the food chain which supports them.

STONE WALLS

Till within the last sixty years there was no communication between any of these vales by carriage-roads: all bulky articles were transported on pack-horses. Owing, however, to the population not being concentrated in villages, but scattered, the valleys themselves were intersected as now by innumerable lanes and pathways leading from house to house and from field to field. These lanes, where they are fenced by stone walls, are mostly bordered with ashes, hazels, wild roses, and beds of tall fern at their base: while the walls themselves, if old, are overspread with mosses, small ferns, wild strawberries, the geranium and lichens. It is a great advantage to the traveller or resident, that these numerous lanes and paths, if he be a zealous admirer of Nature, will lead him on into all the recesses of the country so that the hidden treasures of its landscape may, by an eveready guide, be laid open to his eyes.

William Wordsworth's *Guide to the Lakes*, 1808

It is not the stones in stone walls that make the habitat, but the gaps between them. There are the mosses, the lichens; plants which grow out of the cavities such as the ivy-leaved toadflax and spur valerian, polypody and the usual variety of ferns. Then there are the myriad insects which shelter in the gaps: spiders, flies, midges, beetles, hibernating moths and butterflies, snails and slugs. All of these, whilst favouring the gaps, also favour the different geological materials from which the walls are built. Small birds such as blue tits and wrens often nest in them; they are one of the favourite roosting places for birds of prey, which are all too aware of the mice, shrews, voles, weasels, rats, stoats and moles also living in the walls. Going up the food chain, rabbits, hares, badgers and foxes all find shelter in stone walls and hedgerows. And, of course, squirrels take great delight in hiding their stores of nuts in the gaps in a stone wall.

A dead tree left in a hedgerow.

The plants which colonize a stone wall can be a clue as to its age. When new plants move in they often wipe out their predecessors and become so well established that no other plants can take root in the wall. This is often true of pellitory-of-the-wall, which is found on walls which date back to monastic times.

THE HEDGEROW REGULATIONS

At long last, on 1st June 1997, the Hedgerow Regulations came into being. They lay out quite clearly the criteria for defining whether a hedgerow is deemed 'important' and therefore protected by law. I think it appropriate to reproduce the Regulations in full here (see opposite page), as they provide a good definition of the ancient hedgerows that form such an important part of green lanes.

IMPORTANT HEDGEROWS: THE CRITERIA

The Department of the Environment's Regulations specify in detail the criteria for evaluating whether a particular hedgerow is deemed 'important' and therefore protected by law. This is a simplified guide.

1. Marks a pre-1850 parish or township boundary.
2. Incorporates an archæological feature.
3. Is part of, or associated with, an archæological site.
4. Marks the boundary of, or is associated with, a pre-1600 estate or manor.
5. Forms an integral part of a pre-Parliamentary enclosure field system.
6. Contains certain categories of species of birds, animals or plants listed in the Wildlife and Countryside Act or Joint Nature Conservation Committee (JNCC) publications.
7. Includes:
   (a) at least 7 woody species, on average, in a 30 metre length;
   (b) at least 6 woody species, on average, in a 30 metre length and has at least 3 associated features;
   at least 6 woody species, on average, in a 30 metre length, including a black-poplar tree. or large-leaved lime, or small-leaved lime, or wild service-tree: or
   (d) at least 5 woody species, on average, in a 30 metre length and has at least 4 associated features.

The number of woody species is reduced by one in northern counties. The list of 56 woody species comprises mainly shrubs and trees. It generally excludes climbers (such as clematis, honeysuckle and bramble) but includes wild roses.

8. Runs alongside a bridleway, footpath, road used as a public path, or a byway open to all traffic and includes at least 4 woody species, on average, in a 30 metre length and has at least 2 of the associated features listed at (i) to (v) below.

The associated features are:

(i) a bank or wall supporting the hedgerow;
(ii) less than 10% gaps;
(iii) on average, at least one tree per 50 metres;
(iv) at least 3 species from a list of 57 woodland plants;
(v) a ditch;
(vi) a number of connections with other hedgerows, ponds or woodland; and
(vii) a parallel hedge within 15 metres.

Produced by the Department of the Environment

A hedgerow showing an animal run.

Badger Lane, showing how resourceful these animals can be.

An estimated 100,000 miles (160,000 km.) of hedge have disappeared over the last ten years, but hedgerows are now protected against further destruction. In Yorkshire recently, a man called Colin Seymour saved a local hedge from becoming a bowling green and as a result became a local hero. (In the next chapter there is an example of where this *didn't* happen in Leicester.)

In regard to the preservation of hedgerows, there are one or two things to look out for. Firstly, if a hedge is to be cut by machinery, make sure this does not occur during the nesting season in spring. A hedge which is cut down to less than five feet (1.5 metres) is of little use to wildlife, just as one which has grown over six and a half feet (2 metres) will find its hedgerow trees becoming 'standards' (young trees that are left to mature), and the rest of the hedge becoming gappy.

GREEN LANE VERGES

There are some counties in which the verges seem to be a more prominent feature of lanes than the hedgerows. Where a lane is over thirty yards wide, the variety of flora is often more akin to a meadow habitat than to the woodland of a hedgerow. The grassland habitat of the byway from Castleton at Shocklach to Wetreins Green and beyond (mentioned in the previous chapter) has led to the lane being designated as a Grade B Site of Biological Interest.

There are other green lanes with wide verges which run through chalkland, producing an abundance of flowers from the cornflower and poppy families. At Middleton on the Pennine Way, a rare species of violet, primroses, pansies, saxifrages and the rare blue gentian are to be found.

CONSERVATION

One of the central arguments of this book is that, in order for green lanes to remain open, they need to be used; only in this way will they be prevented from disappearing from our landscape. However conservationists see this as a danger, for more use by humans will inevitably lead to less use by wildlife. With this in mind, it would surely be possible to designate certain green lanes as wildlife havens, and place them on the list of Sites of Special Scientific Interest (SSSI). They would then enjoy a protected status, and could be monitored as they grew into small woodlands and shelter belts over the years. A lasting record of each type of lane could be made by protecting those which ran through different kinds of habitats in every county: wetland, woodland, coastal and heathland. They would be closed to the public, being available only to those animals which used them and lived in them. The only 'human' traffic they would know would be imaginative—such as Kenneth Grahame's Toad in *The Wind in the Willows*, tearing down the centre of the lane in his motor car.

RIGHT Green lanes which run through different habitats, in this case woodlands and meadows, have a corresponding variety of flora and fauna.

Chapter Six

PATHWAYS FOR PROVISIONS

Drovers' Roads & Packhorse Trails

DROVERS' ROADS AND PACKHORSE TRAILS

A name's but a fetter. And I'm a rover
But failing a better
I'm called Hugh the Drover.

From Ralph Vaughan Williams' romantic ballad opera *Hugh the Drover*, libretto by Harold Child

Human travel was first prompted by basic needs, of which the transport of food is one of the most significant. I ask you therefore to think of drovers' roads and packhorse trails as the forerunners of our motorways. Ancient trails used for carrying provisions often also took direct routes to reach their destinations: just as lorries make for out-of-town hypermarkets, so did droves of cattle make for out-of-town sites for fairs or fattening-up sites, avoiding any towns which lay on the routes.

The distances over which comestibles were transported depended on their perishability. Salted butter could be transported further than fresh butter; cheese lasted even longer. For them to remain fresh, vegetables and fruit must always have been distributed to local markets. In the main, packhorses were carrying basic commodities (and illegal luxuries), whereas the drovers took charge of livestock which needed to be taken to market. This gave rise to two distinct types of lane: the packhorse path and the drovers' road. These were not mutually exclusive, for different forms of transport will have used each and every lane over the period of its existence.

As the most important period for long-distance droving was between 1750 and 1850, let us first go back to earlier times, to take a look at some of the older established packhorse paths.

Whereas it would not have been considered necessary to surface a drovers' way, and indeed it would have been for the welfare of the cattle that such ways remained stone-free, this was not the case for packhorse trails. Many of these still retain their metalled surfaces, dating back to Roman times, in the form of stone slabs or steps. Near Hollinsclough in the High Peak there is a section of paved track running over the Axe Edge into the Goyt Valley.

The most famous packhorse ways belong to the North of England. In Derbyshire there is a lane which runs from Brough to Hathersage near Sheffield which has been cut ten feet down into the limestone. This seems to be a testament to the fury with which the packhorse trains of the time must have thundered through the gorge, as there are examples of lanes, dating back to Saxon times at least, which were formed on limestone strata and have not sunk at all.

Some packhorse ways retain their old names, such as the Old Packhorse Road from Grasmere to Ullswater.

> ...The rapidity with which these animals descend the hills, when not loaded, and the utter impossibility of passing loaded ones, require that the utmost caution should be used in keeping out of the way of the one, and

LEFT: Aldwynkle Lane in Northampton, a typically wide drovers' road.

A packhorse path didn't need to be so wide as a drovers' lane. (Culvetor Lane, Devon)

Quakers Causeway in Teesdale, showing a paved causeway for packhorses. These stone surfaces prevented the hooves from slipping.

exertion in keeping ahead of the other. A cross way fork in the road or gateway, is eagerly looked for as a retiring spot to the traveller, until the pursuing squadron, or heavy loaded brigade, may have passed by. In these lanes it is absolutely impossible to form any idea of the surrounding country, as the size and depth of the abutting fields are only to be seen through a breach in the mound, over a stile or gateway.

In the Lake District we are still able to find examples of green lanes which were packhorse ways, as it was here that many roads were only ever passable for one horse. The coming of the turnpikes did not affect them; they remained as minor ways, and some have now been taken over as recreational routes.

The turnpikes thrived during the Industrial Revolution in the Pennines, where many of the first mills were sited; and although they run at heights above the valleys, the lanes survived longer by being used by those who did not wish to use the valley-bound turnpikes.

Of the many schemes devised to halt the thundering of the packhorses, especially when they were approaching bridges, one of the the simplest is the zigzag in the road, which would slow down their advance. Some bridges which we would not today count as belonging to the packhorse age still have stretches of road leading to them which are of a zigzag nature, revealing their earlier origins. Sometimes a 'stopping bar' served to check their speed when coming down a steep slope, often in the form of a natural ridge which was made to intrude above the surface of the lane and cause the packhorses to break their step.

Packhorse trains could comprise between forty and fifty ponies, all jingling along to warn travellers coming in the opposite direction of their approach. The routes did not need to be of great width, although they sometimes followed the ancient wide prehistoric trackways of the region. But it is this sunken effect which is most associated with packhorse trails (and especially with smugglers' ways), and with what was ironically referred to as 'free trade'.

And if you hear a whistle call
All softly in the lane.
Don't pop your head out through the door,
Nor through the window pane.
For you heard nothing,
For owls were in the trees,
And you heard simply nothing else,
Just nothing, if you please.
(The owls that call round Smoky House,
About the roof of Smoky House,
Round golden thatched old Smoky House)
Long live Free Trade!

From *Blue Mountain* by Elizabeth Goudge

Everyone knows of a smugglers' path near the coast. In some counties, especially those in the south-west of England, many a tale of adventure, excitement and quick profit linger round the existence of a green lane leading down to the coast or a river estuary. The packhorses using them were not carrying basic commodities for, as the records for paths around Staithes in North Yorkshire show, besides spirits there were playing cards, silk, spinning wheels, tea, chocolate, pepper and snuff to be had. In order to avoid the Revenue Men, the packhorses often had their hooves covered in cloth so that no noise was heard on their escape up from the beach. One smugglers' path which does not run close to the coast but bears this name is on the ridgeway between Hod and Hambledon Hills near Shaftesbury. It does however follow the pattern of lanes which run from west to east from a coastal area towards a major town, in this case London.

Drovers' roads coming downhill, showing 'stemming stones' to halt the precipitous rush of cattle.

One of the most attractive smugglers' paths in the West Country is to be found at Ringmore. The local pub, now known as Journey's End, had a secret room where contraband was hidden; the smugglers managed to escape detection by the Revenue Men as the pub was the meeting place of the Town Council. In 1685 (then named the New Inn) it was described as "a house of good order with no cards or dice to be found".

The restricted, tunnel effect which these green lanes create has been likened to marriage, in a poem entitled *A Devonshire Lane*, written by the Reverend Marriott of Dartmoor in the nineteenth century:

In a Devonshire lane, as I trotted along
'Tother day, much in want of a subject of song,
Thinks I to myself, I have hit on a strain,
Sure marriage is much like a Devonshire lane.

In the first place 'tis long, and when you are in it,
It holds you as fast as a cage does a linnet;

For however rough and dirty the road may be found,
Drive forward you must, there is no turning round.

In the rock's gloomy crevice the bright holly grows
The ivy waves fresh o'er the withering rose,
And the evergreen love of a virtuous wife
Soothes the roughness of care, cheers the winter of life.

Then long be the journey, and narrow the way,
I'll rejoice that I've seldom a turnpike to pay:
And whatever others say, be the last to complain,
Though marriage is just like a Devonshire lane.

What of the ponies themselves? There are eight breeds of pony in the British Isles that are named after the various areas where they are to be found: Dartmoor, Dale, Fell, Highland, New Forest, Shetland, Connemara and Exmoor. These evolved in their turn from the three hundred breeds of horses which are to be found in western Europe.

For example, the pure Exmoor of today is descended from Celtic chariot ponies and Cornish pack ponies, which in turn have been permitted to interbreed freely with the ponies which run on Dartmoor. The Exmoor ponies are hardy creatures, which were used to carry up to three hundredweight (150 kg.) of goods and, in flat country, were able to cover up to twenty-five miles (40 km.) a day. 'Jaggers' (an old breed of packhorse pony) were popular in the Peak district, along with the Galloway Jagger crosses. The men in charge of the trains were known as 'jaggers'.

As for the panniers that were used, they seemed to have taken many forms. The illustrations on pages 88 and 90 show barrels and specially constructed boxes with removable bottoms being used in the transportation of lime. No doubt removable and false bottoms were used on those beasts which trudged the smugglers' paths. In her *Journal of Rides throughout Britain*, written in the eighteenth century, Celia Fiennes commented on the height of the 'crooks' or 'crubs' in Devonshire, which were used to transport goods; she said they were of three different sizes according to what was being transported. These panniers were designed to clear the sides of the particularly narrow lanes in the West Country. Where packhorses trod moorland paths, as width was not an obstacle, the packs themselves could be much wider. An interesting feature of some lowland lanes is that they are narrower at ground level than at the height of the panniers, which ensured that the packs would not be damaged by rubbing against the sides of the lane.

A packhorse wending its way through a green lane. Packhorse trains would herald their approach by the jingling bells attached to their harnesses.

For every packhorse way there were packhorse bridges, as particular care had to be taken at river crossings. Although much has already been written about early bridge construction, just think how devastating it could have been to lose a well-earned load to the water because of the weakness of a bridge.

The term 'packhorse bridge' is nowadays often applied to any narrow bridge which stands on a minor road, yet many of our major bridging points began life as packhorse bridges. The most picturesque of them are to be found in Cumbria and Derbyshire. Although some of these comply with the guideline concerning the dating of a bridge by the height of its parapets (see Chapter One), some of these bridges (for example Slater's Bridge in Little Langdale) date back to the Industrial Revolution and the heavier use of the packhorse ways.

In the south of England, the packhorse bridges were not generally built with high spans, presumably because the spates were not so extreme. On the drovers' and packhorse routes from Farnham to Guildford stands a series of bridges built in mediæval times: the Tilford East and North Bridges, and another two at Lower Eashing. The documentation relating to the building of bridges would often stipulate whether they should be usable for horses, in which case they were to be five feet three inches wide; if for carts, they were to be eleven feet wide.

Preempting bridge construction, stretches of road immediately either side of a river crossing (sometimes referred to as 'causeys' or causeways) had to be maintained. The following extract from Rev. Gilbert White's *Antiquities of Selborne* (1788) reports on repairs which were made to the then green lane which led to the Fair:

> This vicar (Gilbert White) also gave by will two hundred pounds towards the repairs of the highways in the parish of Selborne. That sum was carefully and judiciously laid out in the summer of the year 1730, by his son John White, who made a solid and firm causey from Rood Green, all down Honey lane, to a farm called Oak Woods, where the sandy soil begins. This miry and gulfy lane was chosen as worthy of repair, because it leads to the forest, and thence through the Holt to the town of Farnham in Surrey, the only market in those days for men who had wheat to sell in this neighbourhood. This causey was so deeply bedded with stone, so properly raised above the level of the soil, and so well drained, that it has, in some degree, withstood fifty four years of neglect and abuse; and might, with moderate attention, be rendered a solid and comfortable road.

Chislecombe bridge on Exmoor.

At Coombe Bissett in Wiltshire, close to the Ridgeway and to a Roman road which runs into Salisbury, two bridges stand (one of which is known as the Packhorse Bridge). There are stone arches on the downstream side only.

The magic of the packhorse bridge reminds me of the following passage from Italo Calvino's *Invisible Cities*. It is a conversation between two great travellers, Kubla Khan and Marco Polo.

> Marco Polo describes a bridge, stone by stone. "But which is the stone that supports the bridge?" Kubla Khan asks.

"The bridge is not supported by one stone or another," Marco answers "but by the line of the arch that they form."

Kubla Khan remains silent, reflecting. then he adds: "Why do you speak to me of the stones? It is only the arch that matters to me." Polo answers. "Without stones there is no arch."

'BADGERS' AND 'HIGGLERS'

There were two main types of dealers who dealt with perishable produce, the 'badgers' and the 'higglers'. The latter dealt in poultry and eggs, which they obtained direct from the farmers' wives. The higglers would sometimes deal by exchanging mugs and utensils for the poultry and eggs which they received.

'Badgers' were the middlemen for the corn trade, and occasionally for butter and cheese. They were an interesting group of travellers, who must have been very familiar with these green trackways. They had to be registered officially at Quarter Sessions and be married gentlemen or women.

There were quite a few more women dealing in this way towards the second half of the nineteenth century, as this chart shows.

	1831	1841	1851
Hawker (male)	9,457	11,099	16,517
(female)	3,563	9,230	(n/a)

Harrison, writing in *Of Faires and Markets 1577-87*, complains that "the richer farmers took to buying up all corn as security for their wealth." They were also known to take on a 'badger' to buy stock for them at market anonymously until their lofts were full. Likewise, he blames the rise in the price of butter upon the 'buttermen' and states that an estimate of each man's corn

The Grundle at Stanton in Suffolk. This impressive holloway, once a millers' path and drovers' road, is at least 25 feet deep in places. Tracks run along the sides and on the bottom.

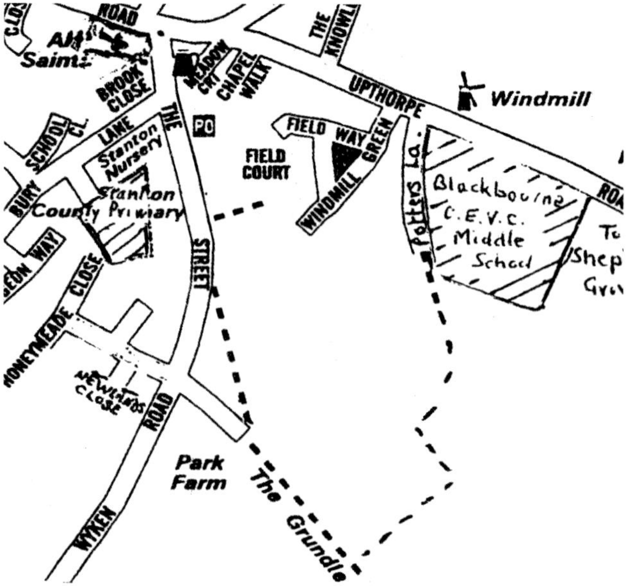

Map showing the position of the Grundle (at foot of map) on one of Suffolk's 'windmill trails'.

Shindle Mill near Salcombe, with a sunken path as access, which still remains green today.

should be made after every harvest. He sees the many middlemen as being the cause of the increase in prices. Some attempt was made to restrict them by not permitting them to bid in open market until it had been going for a full hour. For anyone interested in this field, lists of badgers' licensing records are readily available in Records Offices; these will provide their names and dwelling places, from which further research can be attempted.

By looking at the lanes which survive in one small area, the farms to which they lead, their dates and the markets they were providing, a pattern of green lanes may emerge. The names of the farmers, if still found locally, sometimes survive in a district as carriers and subsequently hauliers.

From this time onwards, the study of packhorse routes becomes very much a local matter, based on what goods were available locally and a consideration of specialist markets. Here is information on two or three of these, which are of local interest and deal with flour, one of the badgers' main commodities.

A flour way existed from Goring to Henley, part of which is now a green lane. The flour was being shipped up into London and stored in the City of London.

> Inquiry of the Privy Council and reply of the Lord Mayor concerning the food supply of the City of London 23rd March 1574.
> What Quantitie hath bene usually for the most part kepte in your Garners?
> We say there hath bene kept comenlie in the garneres and bridgehouses of the Citie's provision some yeres 1200 and some yeres 1500 quarters, which was converted into meale to serve and furnyshe the markets.

With these flour routes, we are obviously dealing with lanes which could accommodate carts as well as packhorses.

In seeking green lanes which were used to transport provisions by packhorse or cart there are, of course, a wealth of millers' paths, lanes and roads to be found. There is a lost Miller's Road just north of Clare in Cambridgeshire. Also associated with the harvest are those known as 'truss ways', this referring to the bundling up of produce.

At Parson Drove in Suffolk there is evidence that the Romans took over the already established practice of milling woad. It was grown hereabouts by the ancient Britons to provide them with their war paint; its purplish colour proved equally popular with their conquerors. The mills attached to this product have long since gone, and the fields are no longer used for growing woad, but the lanes hereabouts all bear evidence of droving days and sometimes to the breed of cattle—for example there is a Black Drove here, which could refer to the black Welsh or

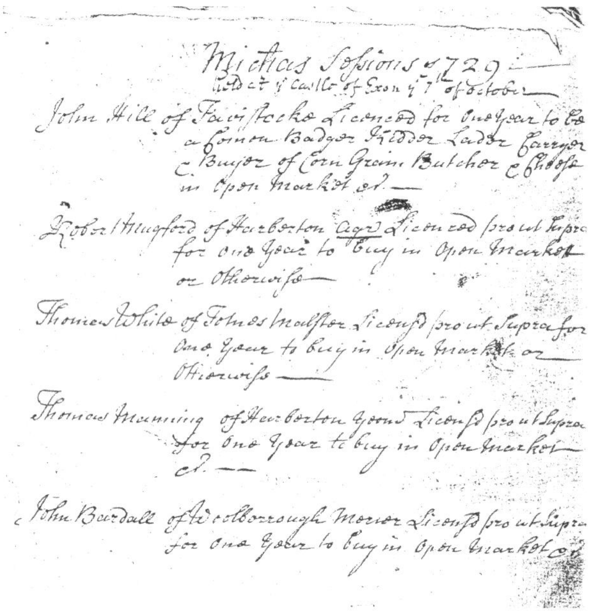

Michas Sessions 1729
held at ye Castle of Exon ye 7th of October
John Hill of Tavistocke Licensed for one Year to be a Comon Badger Kidder Lader Carryer & Buyer of Corn Grain Butcher & Cheese in Open market &c —
Robert Hungford of Harberton Lic[en]sed pro ut Supra for one Year to buy in Open Market or Otherwise —
Thomas White of Totnes Malster Licensed pro ut Supra for One Year to buy in Open Market or Otherwise —
Thomas Manning of Harberton Yeoman Licensed pro ut Supra for One Year to buy in Open Market &c —
John Bardall of Woolborough Mercer Licensed pro ut Supra for One Year to buy in Open market &c

From Quarter Session Michaelmas records of 1729, the licensing records of five 'badgers', which gave them the right to trade in corn, grain, butter and cheese for one year.

Packhorses with wooden panniers which had hinged bottoms for easy unloading.

Galloways which were brought here to be fattened up.

Other kinds of provisions were carried through green lanes for the brewing industries, including apples, hops, malt and barley. There are lanes around Hereford used by the cider trade, and others in Kent used by hop-growers. We shall draw the line on provisions here to leave space to discuss one essential item, which almost deserves a chapter all of its own: I refer to the salt of the earth and its distribution.

SALTWAYS

One of the most important commodities to be transported over these pathways for provisions was salt. It was used in the preparation and preservation of food, in medicine and for personal hygiene. The word derives from 'salary', the allowance of salt given to Roman soldiers as part of their wages; and if salt were used as purchasing power then a 'sale' was made.

In looking for evidence of green lanes having once been saltways, place names provide the best clues. Although the ending 'wick' or 'wich' was once associated with any small settlement in Cheshire, in time it came to be solely associated with the salt industry, and this usage spread to any other area where salt was to be found. Alfred Watkins, in *The Old Straight Track*, gives plenty of examples of 'wicks' on ley lines.

W. B. Crump, who made a detailed study of the saltways radiating out from Cheshire, notes that the packhorse ways which transported the goods often veered off from the main routes and wound their way towards their destinations. The main areas where rock salt was obtained were Northwich, Nantwich and Middlewich. Professional salters were involved in the carrying of salt all year round. The industry was originally in ecclesiastical hands, and licences were given to people from

Gloucestershire, Warwickshire and Herefordshire which permitted them to collect salt from Cheshire. The distinctive feature of the Cheshire 'wiches' was that the salt was openly for sale, though the stranger from another hundred or shire would have paid a heavier toll than someone from Cheshire. Tolls were charged according to the size of load: cart loads, horse loads and man loads. The following is an entry from a salt steward's account book (a crannock or krenneke is an unknown quantity).

> June 1586 two krennekes and a halffe of salte at the Northe wyche 35s spent in fetching the same and for that which was paued for towle 3s 4d.

Some other well known saltways are to be found in the following locations: along part of the Earl's Way from Caldon Grange near Ashbourne (GR086468) to Earlsway House in Staffordshire (GR914618); the Saddler's Way in Tegg's Nose, Country Park, Macclesfield, Cheshire; also in Cheshire there is Bank's Lane at Rainow (SJ972765-984766). The bridge between England and Wales over the Dee at Farndon, built by the monks of St. Werburgh's Abbey 650 years ago, was on a well-established saltway.

In Devon on the Teign estuary there is Whitestone, which Watkins tells us aligns with Bovey Tracey Church, Whiteway Wood, Whiteway House and Whiteway Barton. They all align with Coombe Cellars, a famous smuggling site but also one associated with the salt trade since the 14th century. As in all estuary sites, green lanes which lead down to the water still survive. Here is a description of the Essex Marshes:

Essex saltmarsh showing estuary roads used by both sledge and packhorse.

> A roadless land and a houseless land. Down on the marshes the only roads are still the old green, barge roads, those raised and silent trackways which run from upland farm lanes where straw hangs on the hedges and finches scold the weasels, to the hairy sea walls where, on the creek edge, the black piles of an ancient and disused staithe mark where once the barges lay days and nights on end while wheat was loaded or cattle were driven aboard for transport to the mainland.
>
> J. Wentworth Day, *The Coast of Enchanted Wings*

In Essex there are 'salty' place names such as Salcot, Abbot's Wick and Whiteway Hill, all near Tolleshunt D'Arcy; and Eastwick, Bridgewick and Landwick, all near Southminster. The estuary crossings at North and South Fambridge, also near Southminster, must have seen the crossing of packhorses carrying salt amongst other commodities. And for those keen to discover even more saltways, 'Red Hills' is another place name related

Martinmas was the Anglo Saxons' bloodmonath (blood-month, the time that the animals were slaughtered), and must have been one of the busiest on these green lanes. A sombre time to travel, for a sombre purpose.

This simple form of carriage was used extensively to transport heavy goods from ports and estuaries to towns and markets. There may be salt or flour in these barrels.

to the salt trade. It refers to the crocks in which the salt water was boiled and from which it was drained. After many years of service, the crocks were broken up and applied to the earth, which was most beneficial for the agriculture which followed.

Finally, let us return to drovers' routes, to show how all these trade routes once depended on each other. The main salting season for beef and pork was from the end of September to the end of March, which were the worst months for travel. (It is interesting to speculate how they managed to keep the salt dry whilst transporting it; it may be that most of it was taken to the customers in the summer months.)

In 1703, fresh meat was issued to sailors in home ports at least once a week. But in 1885, just over a hundred years later, the payments to contractors supplying salted beef to the victualling stores at Deptford, Chatham, Dover, Portsmouth and Plymouth show that over 16,000 cattle were slaughtered for this purpose: a considerable change from fresh to salted meat.

DROVERS' ROUTES

Although the droving trade flourished from 1750-1850, it would be true to say that any unmade farm track still in use today was once used to herd cattle for milking or shelter, and therefore is a drovers' route. On this basis, a register of drovers' ways throughout the country would number in the thousands. However we shall define a droving route as one which was used for the mass movement of cattle over long distances, to provide meat for markets further afield than local ones. This practice took place along prehistoric tracks such as the Icknield Way, whose very name *yken/ychen* means 'oxen', as well as referring to the Iceni tribe.

A study of the formation of an Iron Age hillfort shows a series of grazed pastures lying below the enclosures which top such constructions. The fields where the cattle were grazed were accessible through lanes, so many hillforts dating from this period have access lanes through which cattle were driven.

Along the Icknield Way at Dunstable there is a valley marked with lynchettes (mediæval terracing) which can be easily seen, as chalk underlies the grass. The three other main ancient routes—Watling Street, the Fosse Way and Ermine Street—all contain sections which would have been used by drovers.

Some drovers' routes which still survive do so as short lengths of lane leading to rivers or ports, from which the cattle would have been transported.

Religious houses and monasteries were the great landowners of mediæval times, possessing large flocks of sheep. Fountains Abbey alone had 70,000, and the combined religious houses of Yorkshire grazed 200,000 between them. Before the Industrial Revolution, the need to transport these sheep was restricted to taking them to local fairs, so short distance droves developed; these often ran along existing inter-monastic cartularly routes. Many of these lanes continued in use well after the Dissolution of the Monasteries.

The movement of cattle and sheep between winter and summer pastures also gave rise to the creation of drovers' lanes. This is a practice known as 'transhumance', described as such because those who cared for the cattle would have to leave their homes and take up temporary residence with the beasts in the summer months on higher pastures, where the grass would be lusher. In 1691 an Act of Parliament was passed which set out that 'driftways' (or drovers' roads) were for foot and horse traffic only, and were to be three feet wide; whereas a 'cartway' had to be up to eight feet wide. This seems a particularly strange piece of legislation, which must have been made by a town dweller, for the main characteristic of a drove road was its width, as the illustrations in this chapter show. The original drovers' ways belong to times when there were no restrictions placed by landowners or highway authorities over the routes that were taken by travellers; the roads were constructed to accommodate different weather conditions and the

Watling Street at Crick, Northamptonshire, running parallel to the M1 motorway (in the background), the main railway line and a turnpike which once echoed only to the sound of cattle and drovers' cries.

proximity of markets, fairs and ports.

When running along ridgeways, these ancient drovers' routes would be bleak and open; when the cattle were moved via holloways, they would be sunken and sheltered. Some have survived today because they followed routes which were independent of the turnpikes, in order to avoid paying tolls. Some disappeared when the Enclosure Acts incorporated them into new field systems. As wheeled transport increased during the peak period for drovers, there must often have been conflicting interests. Take the recorded case of ten thousand eggs being transported from Cumberland to London, all packed safely in rows of straw and loaded into carts. The prospect of suddenly meeting a 300-strong herd of cattle along the way would have been enough to warrant a request for an early 'No Thoroughfare for Cattle' sign.

But what of the drovers themselves?

Chapter Six

THE DROVERS

Place name evidence for drovers' routes can be as obvious as this.

The Bishopstone-Heathfield droveway crossing the Downs in East Sussex.

These seem to have been a class of labouring middlemen. By 1750, most farmers were not selling their cattle straight from their farms, but were entrusting them to a drover. The Welsh drovers in particular were trusted in this way, whereas the Scottish drovers would already have purchased their animals before they set out on their journeys to the Midlands or London. Bills of credit were used in these transactions, rather than money. The term 'jobber' was used in connection with droving; these were the men who would often take over from the drover when the actual selling was about to take place at market. A drover would be in charge of between fifty and sixty beasts, and his wages would be in the region of double that of the farm labourers of the day. Droves themselves would not amount to more than two hundred cattle, so a head drovesman would be in charge of several groups of cattle and drovers. They would need to be resourceful, for their cattle as well as themselves, having to deal with all sorts of weather conditions, illness in the beasts, and difficulties in finding fresh grazing fields. They did not often sleep out with the cattle, but rather made for 'stances', 'halts', 'lairages' or 'booths', where the cattle would rest up. The timing of this must have been learned from bitter experience, one imagines, for cattle only covered on average twelve miles (20 km.) a day in high terrain, and twenty to twenty-five near London, where the going got smoother. The drovers were helped by dogs; these were so well-trained that they were able to return home from the fairs on their own. There was no droving on Sundays, and as a result many markets took place on a Monday. The droves rested twice a day, and often for a whole day out of every three travelled, depending on the conditions.

Celia Fiennes, writing in her diaries in the seventeenth century, records that London could be virtually cut off from the North by the belt of clays which stretch across the Midlands. The meat supplies to London would be low in wet winters. She states that Watling Street at Hockley in the Hole (now known as Hockliffe) was a "sad road" because of this. Besides being amateur vets, the drovers would also have to carry a supply of shoes, and be able to shoe the beasts if necessary.

There was the constant threat of being mugged, so few stayed out in the open; inns, barns and established farms where stances were available were preferred.

THE DRIVEN

Nowadays, cattle arriving at an abattoir weigh between 65 and 90 stone. About a hundred and fifty years ago, they would have weighed around 48 stone, and two hundred years ago between just 11 and 14 stone! Weight loss during the journey to market (the last stage before the trip to the abbatoir) in the eighteenth century could be as much as four stone per beast, as the rich grazing pastures of the agrarian revolution had yet to develop.

Four main breeds of cattle were driven from Scotland: Ayrshire, Polled Aberdeen Angus, Galloways and West Highland. Of these, the last two were the most popular, and also the most hardy. The two main breeds in Yorkshire were Holderness and Craven, and from Wales came the small black cattle such as the Castle Martins. They were all hardy beasts, with thick coats able to withstand such long journeys.

We have seen that droves consisted of approximately two hundred cattle. What kind of a price was the drover to pay, if he travelled on a turnpike road? He would also have had to pay for the shoeing of the horses before they left; some blacksmiths must have made a lucrative living from this operation. (At The Traveller's Rest outside Cambridge, a quantity of shoes was found which bears this out.)

In the 1750s, some 600,000 sheep were driven into Smithfield Market each year, coming from many places in the north and south of England. Cistercian monks had been amongst the first to develop large-scale sheep farming, mainly for wool. This had given rise to short-distance paths used by shepherds, which later led into the main droving ways throughout the country.

Turkeys and geese were also driven, mainly from East Anglia. Geese were easier to drive as they could eat 'on the hoof'! But turkeys demand special feeds, and trees to roost in at night. There were many local Goose or Goosey Fairs, such as the ones at Tavistock and Nottingham. The geese which were driven to the Leadenhall Markets in London set out from East Anglia in August, arriving by the end of October. Poultry was a high-priced luxury in the eighteenth century, unlike today. A misericord end in Beverley Minster depicts a goose being shod; however it is far more likely that they were made to walk through a mixture of tar, sand and sawdust before setting out. As many as 20,000 geese were driven to Nottingham every year, and it would have taken quite some time to shoe such a large number.

Pigs were driven from Wales to Bristol, and from Cornwall to London, being taken there by 'pig-jobbers' through Dorset along 'hog-ways'; others came from Ireland. The most famous breeds of pigs came from Berkshire, Herefordshire and the Midlands. When driven, the pigs were often muzzled to prevent them grubbing up the lanes, and sometimes they went 'stocking-trottered'. This form of footwear was not unlike modern slippers, as the stockings had built-in leather soles.

THORNS FROM THE NORTH

It would be nice to think that we English could blame the Scots and the Welsh for sending their cattle to us bristling with thistles, which then became transplanted into our lush, lady's smocked meadows—and maybe we can, for it would be difficult to disprove. When studying the flora of drovers' routes, we are confronted with the problem of knowing which species were colonized by which breeds of cattle.

If we recollect the ways in which seed disbursal takes place, any one of them could apply to a drovers' or

HOW TO IDENTIFY GREEN LANES WHICH WERE ONCE DROVERS' WAYS

This checklist will help in identifying such lanes on the ground, but further research will need to be undertaken to be sure that they were once used by drovers. As always, exact dating is difficult, but the most important period for droving was 1750-1850.

Appearance

1. *Width*: this can be from twenty to forty yards.
2. *Stances* or *halts*. These can occur within a lane itself or adjacent to the lane. They will be where the lane horns out to provide a grazing area.
3. The lane will have *very wide tree-free verges* which were also used for grazing. In Yorkshire it has been calculated that there were a hundred acres of pasture available for cattle on the drovers' route from Scotch Corner to Bowes.
4. A *walled or hedged cattle pound* may appear within or at the end of the lane.
5. The *length* of a drovers' way is usually *over half a mile*, but smaller, earlier ways were used for cattle too.
6. The green lane may well *link up with a major road* which leads into a town, e.g. Banbury Lane.
7. It may run *parallel*, sometimes hidden, *to an old turnpike route*, *enclosure road or another major route*.
8. It will *lead in the direction of a market town or former fair, an ecclesiastical institution, or a port.*
9. There will be *some form of water supply adjacent or within the lane*: a natural pond, dewpond, well, spring, or more unusually a trough and a pump.
10. Lane *crosses a natural ford* at a wide point in a river with wide banks.
11. The presence of *Scots Pines* along the way indicated that the landowners were well disposed to offer hospitality to the Scottish drovers.
12. *Smallish, early bridges at minor rivers*, known as packhorse bridges ('hebbles' in Derbyshire)—see main text.

Place name evidence

1. The use of *drove, drift, oxway, the rothern, lode, neat, droveden, the holloway or the shieling* for the lane or roads nearby.
2. Farmsteads along the way may bear such *obvious names as the Halt or Drovers' Rest.*
3. The *fields* within these farms may then be investigated. The following will give evidence of the fees charged by the farmer for grazing. (But they may also refer to the size and value of the field): *Half penny, Farthing, Penfold, Pinfold,* and *Booths* in the Vale of Edale, Derbyshire.
4. *Public houses and inns* also reveal the presence of drovers, such as *The Shepherd and Dog, The Drovers' Arms, The Black Bull and The Fiddlers*—a popular way for Scottish drovers to pass the time. They were also said to knit as they went but I do not know of any hostelry called 'Knit One Pearl One'. Place name evidence may also appear incorporating geese or hogs, e.g. *The Boar's Head.*
5. Names such as *The Blacksmith's Arms* or *The Farrier* also show their presence; and look out for *The Old Smithy* as a private house name. The same applies for evidence of tanneries. As in 4 above, it is the position of these pubs which will reveal their use to drovers: for example *The Travellers Rest* at Epping Green is situated strategically outside the London markets and within early morning striking distance of Epping itself.
6. One of the longest shots to provide evidence of drovers is to be found in the *hair which was used to bind lath and plaster together* in old barns by the wayside. Is the hair of a Highland Welsh or Yorkshire breed?

Written evidence

Trade Directories
(available in most large local libraries and published yearly).
Newspaper Advertisements.
Archive photographs.
Tithe Maps (Records Office) for field names.

packhorse way. The illustrations on pages 70 & 71 give a sample of the flora to be found at various levels along a lane, and are mainly taken from Devon. The only real evidence which can be identified is in regard to the movement of cattle into and out of green lanes from their grazing fields: seeds on their coats would become dislodged on contact with the gateposts, which accounts for the variety of wildflowers in such places. If a number of cattle died along a drovers' route and were buried there, the site would likely be marked by a large patch of stinging nettles, thriving on the nitrates. This, along with place name evidence (where a lane is known as a 'murrain' or 'murrian'), provides conclusive proof of such a lane's funereal history.

EPPING LONG GREEN LANE

On a bright day in early December I stopped at The Traveller's Friend at Epping Green for information, but perhaps I should have just taken that offered by a hovering kestrel, who already knew what I was seeking: a green lane where wildlife live on many levels, and where formerly wild creatures were driven through on their way to London from as far away as Galloway. For this lane was once a drovers' road; geese, ducks, cattle and Galloway ponies rested in the open commons which horn out into this lane to a width of as much as forty yards in some places. The geese were taken to Epping; sometimes they were sold there, or kept overnight on Bell Common before being moved on to the markets on Wanstead Flats and sold on to the market dealers ('higglers') from the Old Goose Yard behind the High Street on the west side. What is now known as Summer's Farm could be a corruption of sumpter, a packhorse driver. The packhorses were taking wool from East Anglia to Waltham Market.

The green parts of the lane are separated by a 300-yard stretch of tarmac in the middle of its length. Under the Epping Forest Act of 1878, the green lanes were preserved, and are now administered by the Corporation of the City of London.

The lane begins in a straggly narrow way, between some unthinned ashes; some spectacularly grape-like berried whitebeams line this short, constricted section. But soon the lane opens out, and visible on the south side are the banks and ditches of the parish boundary between Epping and Nazeing. In 1229, prior to the creation of the parishes, Henry III passed an act which set up a pattern of little ditches and low hedges to enclose the woods "so that wild beasts might go in and out".

The market in Epping was founded in 1253 and an additional market, for cattle only, was instituted in 1671; this lasted barely a hundred years. Although used as a drovers' way, I think that the lane has probably seen more pilgrims and woodsmen on their way to Waltham than animals on their way to markets. In the eleventh century there were those seeking to be in the presence of a fragment of the Holy Cross that was said to have been brought by Tovi, Canute's standard bearer, from Montacute in Somerset to Waltham. Then, in 1290, with its protective double hedge bank in place, the lane would have seen pilgrims accompanying Queen Eleanor's coffin on its funereal journey from Lincoln to nearby Charing Cross, Waltham being one of the resting places on the route.

Coming out of the easterly end of the lane I froze, as did the fox which had slipped out from under the thorny hedgerow cover to cross the lane. He slid gracefully away under the brambles, disturbing a charm of goldfinches feeding on the vividly coloured berries of Epping Long Green Lane.

Once more there arises the difficulty of placing any one of England's green lanes strictly within a single historical period. The adaptability of this lane has ensured its longevity, and one hopes that its recently acquired protected status will enable it to survive indefinitely, despite the ever-present threat of motorized traffic which roars away here, so close to the capital.

Most lanes are rich in history, as the following example shows. Mr. Emlyn Richards, who has written a book on drovers' roads leading from Wales into England, discovered that a Welsh drover is buried in All Saints' Upland church, Epping:

Underneath
lie the remains of
John Jones
late of Madryn Isaf
in the County of Caernarvon
Drover
who died the 21st day
of November 1835.
Aged 55 years.

Mr. Richards also sent me a copy of a very detailed letter outlining the existence of a former drovers' route at Aylestone near Leicester, which has now become incorporated into the city. It was used by the drovers, who were bringing from 30,000 to 60,000 sheep through this area in the 1730s, to avoid the tolls which were made on other routes. 'P.G.' was the anonymous provider of this information to a Professor Jenkins of Bangor University in the 1940s. It seems that he wanted to remain anonymous, as he was rather ashamed of his part in the destruction of the drovers' route, which he had just discovered. He was the Chairman of the Board of the YMCA in Leicester, who wanted to extend their playing field by incorporating the road into the grounds. They did, and a guilt-stricken "P.G." took a photograph of it before it happened, being all the time aware that:

> "This is a genuine old drovers' road and must have been used by all the Welsh Drovers who travelled to Northampton via Hinckley and Leicester..."

CONCLUSION

Because drovers' routes are often long, and packhorse routes so steep and narrow, it is fairly easy to recognize them on the ground, although in comparison with the details that are often available on other topics from mediæval times, there is little documentary evidence to confirm that droving was the primary use of these lanes.

They evoke the feeling of long distance travel with a definite purpose, of green lanes which were in constant commercial use and which witnessed many dramas as a result. Penelope Lively's excellent children's novel *The Driftway* sees the children of the book making acquaintance with a waggoner, who tells them how he feels about the lane:

> This is an old road, son. Older than you or me, or the houses in this village, or the fields round about, or anything we can see now, or even think about... stands to reason that it's got a few tales to tell. There's been men passing by here, and women, and children, over thousands of years, travellers. And every now and then there's someone does an extra hard bit of living, as you might call it. That'll leave a shadow on the road, won't it?

Chapter Seven

THE LANDSCAPE CHANGED

Green Lanes in the Industrial Age

Had you told prehistoric man, all those chapters ago, that he was living in a man-made landscape, he would not have believed it, although it would have been partly true. Today it is almost universally true, and we can watch the process of change on a day-to-day basis, thanks to earth-moving equipment of the mechanized kind. Before such mechanical aids were invented, all changes that were made were the result of human labour.

Changes in agricultural practice had been shaping the landscape for centuries, but mainly on a small scale. With the arrival of the Enclosure Acts of the eighteenth century, the advance of industrialization and the dawning of the age of transport for all, the land really began to be carved up on a grand scale. Changing agricultural patterns and changes in the industrial landscape meant that people were not travelling along the routes they had used in the past. So what were the consequences for road development during this period?

THE ENCLOSURE ACTS

The heart of the matter is that in order to increase production, fields were enlarged; in the process, the lanes which led to the smaller fields often disappeared, although a few still survive as green lanes. The counties which show the most widespread use of this new system were mainly in areas of the country where it was possible to create large, flat fields for increased agricultural production. According to Hindle, fifty per cent of all the Enclosure Acts that were passed applied to Oxford, Cambridge and Northamptonshire, with smaller percentages in Bedford, Leicester, Yorkshire, the East Riding, Rutland, Lincoln, Notts, Bucks, Berks, Warwicks, Norfolk, Wiltshire, Middlesex, Cumberland, Gloucester, the West Riding, Derby and Westmoreland. You can therefore see that few Acts were passed either in the West Country or in Suffolk, Essex, Kent, Sussex and Surrey, which strived to maintain their woodlands.

During this period, one-fifth of the English countryside changed its appearance; one-fifth of the country lanes now in existence, whether green or not, date from this time. But, ironically, this was also the period when many footpaths and other rights of way disappeared. Old ways, which had perhaps led to water mills, churches and small settlements, were swept aside in these new developments. In some places the old ways were retained, such as in the parish of West Ashby in Lincolnshire. The new enclosure road near Thorpe, on its way to Hemingby, suddenly narrows and incorporates the former lane.

Before looking at some examples of the eighteenth century Enclosure Acts, a brief consideration of those Enclosure Acts which pre-date this movement will also reveal some green lane history. As was mentioned at the end of the 'Meeting the Markets' chapter, the enclosure of mediæval fields had been going on in areas where the land had ceased to be profitable under the old open field regime. An example can be found at Norton-on-Tees in Cleveland: it is interesting to see what a full record is made of the roads here, and what care was taken not to

LEFT: Peakland industrial landscape showing green lanes still in use at the beginning of this century.

upset those who had previously worked the open fields.

Below is an example of the implementation of an Enclosure Act in Cleveland:

Woodway or Durham Road
The common highway street in the North Field called Woodway shall begin at the north east corner of the Preben Garth and end at the gate called Minnibats Gate. We appoint a common highway for carts and carriages in the North Field beginning at Minibats Gate and ending at Maudlau Gate. Also a common highway from Minnibats Gate to Ragbath.

Christmire Way
We order another way in the North Field for carts and carriages from the east end of the Woodway adjoining the Crook dike leading to the allotments in the North Meadows and New Close Howell.

Darlington Way
Shall remain as now, that is over the flat called tofts and dikes in the West Field to Kent Gate and then through the south Field to Ragbath Gate. All cottagers whose allotments lie to the west of Kent Gate shall have ways out of Darlington Way.

The Ragbath footway
A common footway from Stockton Lane near the garth ends at Darlington Way and Ragbath Gate.

New or Cottage Lane
To the Holmes through the cottagers lands and East Field.

Norton to Blakiston footway
Along Christmire Lane.

This Act, dated 1670, shows a great respect for the

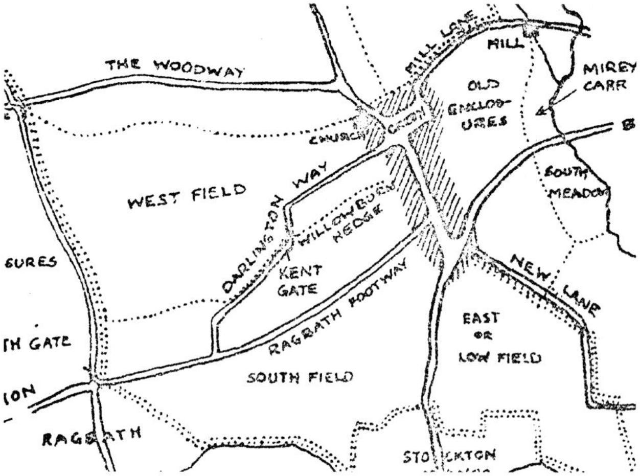

A pre-enclosure map of Norton-on-Tees, c.1670. Field boundaries are marked with single dotted lines; the extent of arable open fields enclosed is marked with a double dotted line.

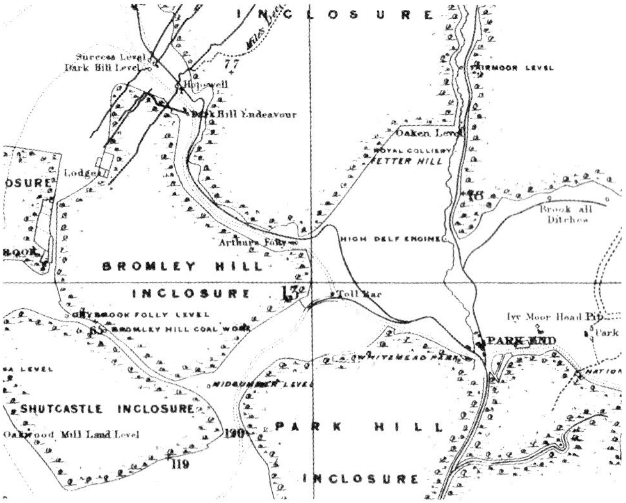

A detail from Sopwith's map of an area in the Forest of Dean dated 1835. It shows the changeover period from the Enclosure lanes, which subsequently became roads connected with an extractive industry, in this case coal and iron.

footways already in existence, which some of the later Acts failed to maintain.

How does this compare with the treatment of highways in the later, larger wave of Enclosure Acts? In 1793 an Act was passed enclosing 675 acres of land in Wadenhoe, Northamptonshire. These are the instructions for the road layout:

> Public Carriage roads to be fenced on both Sides, and no Gates to be erected thereon or Trees planted within 50 yards of each other on either sides thereof.

It goes on to state that "where there is now, or usually hath been a public Road or MEER way... twenty Feet to forty Feet at the least...", it was to be retained or extended so that it linked up with the adjoining parishes. It was a characteristic of enclosure roads that they did not run along parish edges but from field to field, parish to parish. Like the Turnpike Acts, the Enclosure Acts of the 18th Century took on a set form, and did not specify individual considerations.

This is a fine example of a lane which retains its cobbles and camber between the waggon ruts.

A Jolly Waggoner: a sketch by Nigel Wellings from the original in Samuel Smiles' *Lives of the Great Engineers.*

As for the physical construction of the enclosures, this is an account of that from the parish of Raunds, also in Northamptonshire:

> The roads are to be covered with stone 12' wide, being 17' thick in the middle and 5' thick at the outside.

They were to be constructed before further work continued: a commission was put out for people to construct dykes and set double quickset hedges (made of hawthorn bushes), which were to be untouched for seven years.

It seems ironic that these wide lanes should have been created at a time when trade by road was coming under threat from the advent of the canals and railways, as this extract from *The Jolly Waggoner* shows.

> Things is greatly altered now
> And waggons nowhere seen.
> The world's turned topsy-turvey now
> And the things is run by steam.
> And the whole world passes before me
> Just like some morning dream.
>
> Aye things is greatly altered now
> But then what can us do?
> For the folks in power they will take no heed
> Of the likes of me and you.
> It's hardship for us waggoning lads
> And a fortune for the few.

In areas where fields did not exist, the wastes and commons became subject to enclosure, and roads were created to link up these new land divisions. In 1859, at the end of the period of Enclosure Acts, such a road was made on the Fells to the south of Dent, where 'Green Field' runs. It connected Barbondale and Deepdale: two new tracks were created, leading back into the valley.

In Cumbria there are numerous lanes which are listed as once having been Enclosure Roads created to contain the mountain wastes. Another example of an existing highway having been incorporated into an Enclosure Act is to be found in Berkshire on the Old Way from Warbury Camp to Basingstoke (SU559550-564545).

Landlords steadily converted their small estate fields into larger ones by means of Enclosure Acts, but there were other places where Acts were passed because of emergencies. The Napoleonic Wars demanded an increase in production, so larger fields were created to grow more grain for bread production. This was to happen again in the First and Second World Wars.

In Cheshire there is a lane which appears in the Inclosure Award of 1798 as "a private drift and carriage road leading into Lambert's Lane". The following is a list of the documents researched in proving the subsequent age of the road, and is a good guide of what to look for in your area:

County Maps of Cheshire Greenwood 1819, Swire and Hutching 1830, Bryant 1831.
Tithe Map for Congleton 1843.
Ordnance Survey 1st Edition 1872 and Parish Area Book. Ordnance Survey 3rd Edition 1910.
Finance Act 1910 Working Sheet.
Domesday Book, Field Book.
Plan of the Property of W. Reade Esq 1834.
Macclesfield Canal Act 1826.

The last item contains a reference to the road as an "Occupational Road and Public Bridle Road", which brings us on to our next category of green lane.

OCCUPATIONAL LANES AND THOSE USED FOR ACCESS TO MINES

It is good to know that a particular green lane once served a useful function for society. It might have been used for the transportation of coal from the Midlands to London, or for providing a pleasant way homewards for an exhausted, ageing and probably ailing tin miner; at least it was earning its keep. The 'Pathways for Provisions' chapter examined those green lanes which still exist today and were once used for bringing the basic necessities of life to our door. Those above belong to a later time, having brought commodities which made people's lives more comfortable. Such lanes remain as a reminder of when roads were still used for transporting heavy goods, before the canals and railways took over. What remains of them is usually situated very near the

In Cornwall there are the tin mines which are spread throughout the county, both inland and on the coast, nearly always in dramatic positions.

source of the materials being extracted or the goods being provided. Unlike some of the types of lanes we have looked for so far, these are relatively easy to discover, as there may well be some tangible clue as to what they were once used for: old tub-tracks in the centre of a lane for transporting minerals on a simple rack and pinion railway; the remains of iron, tin or lead workings at the end of, or adjacent to, a lane. Once more the names of the lanes will help: Quarry Lane, Tanpits Lane, Lode Lane, etc. Sandy lanes by the sea were also used for transporting seaweed to the slopes nearby for fertilizer.

In Cumbria we have the Borrowdale and Mouthlock Coal Roads in Stainmore Parish. A search for the disused coal fields of Britain will reveal others.

The pits from which iron ore was extracted (and the practice of the ancient art of iron smelting) were to be found in Kent, the Midlands and the Moorland regions of England. In Durham there is the lead-mining trail from Cowshill to Edmundboyers.

Slate quarrier's cottage, now in ruins. This stands at the entrance to a deeply sunken group of lanes where slate was mined from mediæval times until the 1930s.

All along our coasts and estuaries there are lime kilns and the interesting lane networks which led up to them. Routes are named after this industry, such as the Limersgate from Burnley to Rochdale.

Some quarries do not just belong to the age of Industrial Archæology. Near Totnes in Devon there is a group of deeply sunken lanes, forty to fifty feet down, which lead to mediæval slate quarries, holding a secret from another period of history. People who are aware of my interest in ancient lanes often ask me whether I ever feel afraid. Of a living presence?—well that's just the risk you take. Of one which was once of this world and has gone to another but takes the odd awayday back to this one? Only once.

When approaching the slate quarry pits near Totnes, which are a series of very large pools (although their size is such that one could almost call them lakes), I found myself constantly looking over my shoulder to see if I was being followed. Pigs were kept up the the top of the valley—I thought that maybe one was escaping. This happened a few times, and I had no great desire to stay down in the quarry. I mentioned this in conversation with a local historian a few months later, and she told me the following story.

In the days of the Napoleonic Wars, before Princetown Prison was built on Dartmoor to house French prisoners, a group of them was brought to Plymouth. The English officers in charge of them were told that there was nowhere to house them at present, and ordered to see to their disposal. As mentioned, these quarry pits were even then extremely deep and treacherous; the prisoners were murdered and buried there, which explains the apprehension I felt.

Another ancient industry is that of tanning. In South Yorkshire and North Derbyshire there was a thriving tanning industry: over four thousand hides a year were sent down south during the seventeenth century. There are green lanes which lead to the River Don, especially in the Aldwark area. Along with this industry went the mining of alum, which was used in tanning and paper-making—it took fifty tons of shale to produce one ton of alum. In Yorkshire, the main centres were to be found at Guisborough, Littlebeck, Sandsend and Ravenscar.

Pits and mines in this area may have old lanes leading to them. Other products which were mined from them include jet, which is formed from the fossilized remains of waterlogged monkey-puzzle trees. There is a Jet Miners' Track on Cringle Moor which goes round the side of the hills, and in recent years has become incorporated in the Lyke Wake Walk as an alternative route when the weather below is bad. It is to be found on the Cleveland Way.

Still on the North Yorkshire Moors, deposits of ironstone were found at Eston in 1812, and in 1856 rich deposits were discovered in Rosedale. It became a boom town, and many workers walked in from the surrounding hills and villages. However, one of the more unusual lanes in the area is to be found at Rosedale Chimney; it is associated with the miners' recreational activities rather than anything else. It has a 1 in 3 gradient, and was used for hill climbs in the 1920s. The events were part of the programme of the Bradford Motor Cycle and Light Car Club. Arthur Champion (quite naturally) was the winner of the first event: he was a native of Rosedale so had plenty of opportunity to practise. Sections of the lane were even steeper, being 1 in 2½, and stones and tapes were placed to steer riders into this most difficult part. However complaints were made by local residents and it is no longer officially used for this purpose.

In Yorkshire and on the Cleveland Way there is a

series of lanes which for centuries have been used as turbury paths (for transporting peat) into the village of Chop Gate. The nearest car park for access to them is at 558993. Turbury paths are also to be found in other areas of the country, noticeably on Dartmoor and Exmoor.

There is an interesting marrying of the agricultural and the industrial in the west Cornish mining lands, where many a miner built himself a humble dwelling.

The initials GPW, shown above in a green lane outside Scorriton on Dartmoor, stand for German Prisoner of War. These stones belong to the Second World War period, when prisoners were brought in to make good the damage which had been caused to roads in the area by Americans practising in their armoured tanks!

Another kind of green lane which belongs to this period and might merit investigation is that associated with what were known as Rotten Boroughs. By studying the Reform Bills in the first half of the nineteenth century, it will be found that some lanes, which led to villages and towns which were no longer in existence, still had access roads in place. I will leave this for a student of historical geography to research further.

In the 18th century many parts of the countryside would be smoking with working lime kilns, with a ration of one kiln to every four farms. Unfortunately some lime kiln burners, staying on duty by their kilns, would fall in and perish.

INDUSTRIAL MONUMENTS

This is a list of industrial monuments issued by English Heritage. Any one of these sites could have a green lane leading to it which was once, or maybe still is, part of an access and egress route.

There are those leading to extraction sites, mines and quarries such as those for lead, coal, slate, alum, stone, lime, gunpowder, tin, clay, arsenic and barytes; and for the processes leading to the production of glass, iron, steel, brass and cement.

Those leading to sites for the production of electric power, ice (houses), water, sewage treatment, salt, oil, gas and metal workings. Then there are those leading to old engineering sites, i.e. hydraulic rams, disused bridges and early construction sites.

Those which are approach roads to activities in the countryside such as the extraction of inorganic chemicals, organic chemicals, timber, peat production, (turbury paths) rural kilns and those associated with game keeping or hunting.

Activities associated with food production: corn drying and milling sites, brewing and distilling, other organic agricultural products and the textile industry.

Those leading to human, animal, water and wind power, combustion engines, roadways, railways, inland waterways, sea, coast and air transport communications.

And finally, the leisure industry.

The lanes which have been used for transporting minerals are as numerous as the variety of minerals which makes up the earth's surface; and the pursuit of them is of equal length and variety. Happy mineral mapping!

THE TURNPIKE AGE

By 1821 over 18,000 miles (29,000 km.) of English roads had been turnpiked—a turnpike being a toll road set up by a group of merchants to keep the road clear from one market town to another. The word derives from 'turn-spike', which was a pole set up in the road to prevent travellers from passing.

We do not know how many miles of turnpikes are still green lanes; to find out and list them would make a whole book in itself, so once again the search lies at a local level. For the first time in road history we now have a decent body of documentation to back up any field work, although it hasn't always been collected and preserved as it might be: there must still be a lot of turnpike maps languishing in the vaults of shire solicitors and notaries. As a category, turnpike roads will give us the biggest clue as to what might happen to our landscape in the coming years, because they were used for transporting merchandise.

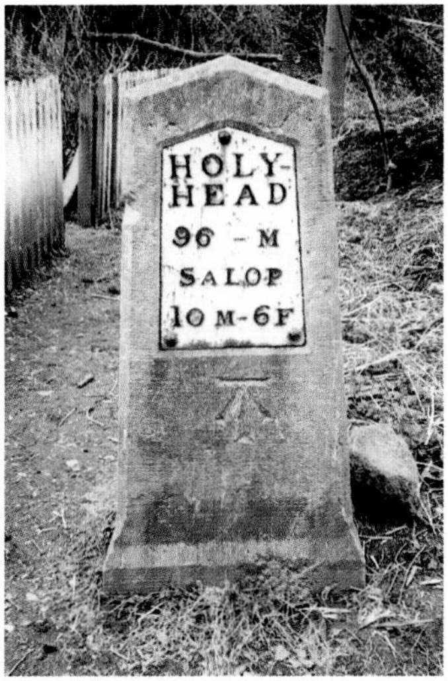

Individually designed by Thomas Telford, the drawings for these milestones can be seen in the Ironbridge Gorge Museum library.

They were once the main routes for wheeled transport, and some have remained so, but the majority have given way to other routes: first the A, B and trunk roads of modern times, and then the motorways.

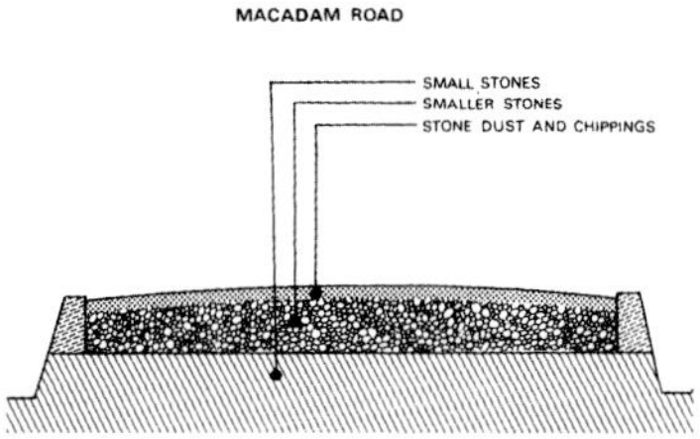

John Loudon Macadam (1756-1836) developed the three-layer system of building roads illustrated here. Many of his roads were turnpiked.

In recent years, many such minor roads have been 'rediscovered', and are now used for recreational purposes. If in the future many of us will be working from home or very locally, will our minor road network bring us in touch again with the reality of travel? There is a certain sense in which cruising along a motorway is travelling without moving: we do nothing to contribute to the journey, we do not interact with the environment through which we are passing. But when we step onto what was once a busy turnpike road, we can be reminded of the difficulties of travel in previous times—no better described than in this

A tollbar placed across a green lane.

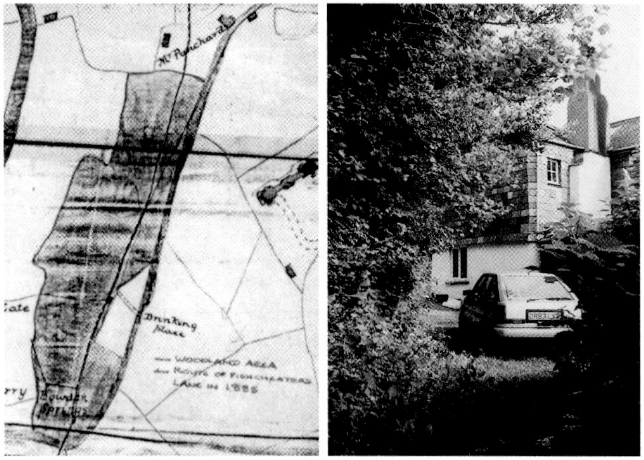

Private map (1885) showing position of Fishcheater's Lane in Totnes, Devon. The map shows the tollhouse which the fish merchants (chowters) would have tried to avoid. This explains the confusion between the words 'cheat' and 'chowter', which produced the word 'fishcheater'.

famous passage of Dickens:

> It was the Dover road that lay, on a Friday night late in November, before the first of the persons with whom this story has business. The Dover road lay, as to him, beyond the Dover mail, as it lumbered up Shooter's Hill. He walked up hill in the mire by the side of the mail, as the rest of the passengers did; not because they had the least relish for walking exercise, under the circumstances, but because the hill, and the harness, and the mud, and the mail, were all so heavy, that the horses had three times already come to stop, besides once drawing the coach across the road, with the mutinous intent of taking it back to Blackheath.
>
> *A Tale of Two Cities (1859)*

Many Turnpike Acts were passed to finance the crossing of the weladen clay in Kent, and some sections survive as green lanes. One such road leads from Deal to

A tollhouse with a green lane running alongside (to its left).

Sandwich, having been opened in the seventeenth century for high speed carriage communication.

Thomas Hardy writes as evocatively as Dickens about road travel; often we see his figures approaching along the dusty road, or waiting for the carrier at a deserted crossroads.

Toll roads are not a new idea: turnpike roads were just that, and they seemed to work well in their early years. They were then superseded by the railways, and their economic development cut short.

There are various characteristics which mark out a green lane as having once been turnpiked. The most obvious is the presence of a tollhouse, a tollbooth or a milestone. In some cases the hedges of the lane may be extra thick in order to keep the travellers within the set route so that they could not avoid paying tolls, but this may alternatively be evidence of a Saxon boundary bank.

The next characteristic will be the surface. As the diagram on the previous page shows, it took a Scotsman to put us right on our road surfaces. For centuries people

A turnpike tollbooth. Unlike tollhouses, these are a great rarity.

had assumed that it was the width and heaviness of the wheels which had to be changed in order to make roads better. John Loudon Macadam, as a result of his travels throughout the United Kingdom, had concluded otherwise, and he developed the three-layered system of road construction which is still in use today.

In some places, the three layers of road built in the era of Macadam still survive: taken together with the Turnpike Trust Accounts and Maps, and the House of Commons Act for the passing of the Turnpike, they will give positive proof of the date of a lane. Some of the most spectacular ex-turnpike roads occur in the North of England and on the Scottish borders. There is the Roman road from

Illustration of paviours from Pyne's *Microcosm* series of 18th century sketches.

Anno viceſimo octavo

Georgii II. Regis.

An Act for repairing and widening the Road from *Chudleigh Bridge*, in the Pariſh of *Hennock*, in the County of *Devon*, through the Town and Borough of *Aſhburton*, to *Brent Bridge*, in the Pariſh of *South Brent*, in the ſaid County.

WHEREAS the Road or High-way leading from a certain Place called Chudleigh Bridge, in the Pariſh of Hennock, in the County of Devon, through the Town and Borough of Aſhburton, to a Place called Brent Bridge, in the Pariſh of South Brent, in the ſaid County, being Nineteen Miles, or thereabouts, lying in the ſeveral Pariſhes of Hennock, Bovey Tracey, Teingraſe, Ilſington, Bickington, Aſhburton, Buckfaſtleigh, Dean Prior, and South Brent, and in the Poſt Road from the City of Exeter, to the Town of Plymouth, in the ſaid County, is become ſo ruinous and bad in the Winter Seaſon, that the ſame cannot, by the ordinary Courſe and Method appointed by the Laws and Statutes of this Realm, be ſufficiently repaired and amended: For Remedy whereof, and to the Intent that the ſaid Road may be well and ſufficiently repaired and amended, and kept in good Repair; May it pleaſe Your Preamb

8 C 2

b

The front page of this Turnpike Act in 1755 shows the route taken by this new road. Those roads which were not covered by such Acts often became green lanes. The very first Turnpike Act in 1663 was from Wadesmill to Royston (now the A1). This was to become known as the Great North Road, sections of which are green lanes today.

A fine stone-faced bank which may have been used by stone-breakers to store the stones they had cracked for use on the turnpike roads.

Ribbleshead to Bainbridge which became turnpiked in 1751; and a section around Dodd Fell, known as Cam High Road. Macadam himself built the section around Shap; where it descends into Crookdale towards Hause Foot Bridge it has become a footpath.

The Roman road from Cam Fell to Bainbridge became turnpiked and is one of the highest green lanes in the country. It runs for seven and a half miles (12 km.) at over 1,500 feet (460 m.) above sea level.

The route from Derby to Manchester was first turnpiked in 1738 but some sections, which used the Roman road surface and were not turnpiked, still survive as green lanes. One of these is a section of the Derby to Buxton road north of Brassington, crossing the White Peak near Pikehall.

Coming south-west, there are a series of holloways which represent the old road from Ross to Kilcot in Herefordshire. From Carey Court there is an overgrown way which lies below the footpath. A sweetly named pub, The Cottage of Content, is in this area.

Let us finish this chapter with the sub-species of de-turnpiked lane known as a carriage run: these would lead from the turnpike up into the privacy of the grounds of the local 'big house'. Sometimes the big house no longer exists, but the carriage run remains as a green lane. One such survives in idyllic conditions near the sea at Wonwell Beach in Devon. The coastal footpath guide for the area reads as follows:

A restored tollhouse, now standing near a road which leads to a present-day roadman's depot.

> Across the stream a grassed-over, one-time carriageway leads off towards a stone building near the path. This was a stable, built to house the horses which drew carriages down to a tea house close by; its foundations can still be seen on the cliff edge. This tea house, part of the Flete Estate, was used for beach parties by the family and their guests who sometimes included members of the Royal Family.

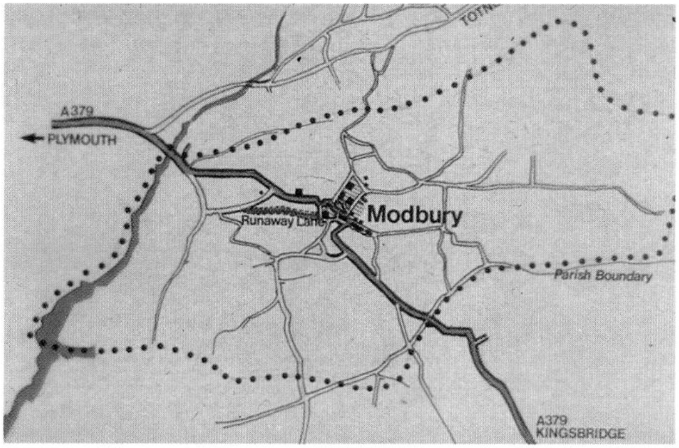

A map showing the position of Runaway Lane at Modbury in Devon.

The Sealed Knot Society re-enacting a battle which dates from the Civil War.

And on that wistful note we will leave behind those green lanes whose hedgerows never smelt the insulting blasts of carbon monoxide, and we shall travel, without moving, into the twentieth century.

I have only traced the many uses for green lanes throughout history up to the Turnpike Age. There are many, many local lanes which have individual stories to tell and which we have no space to list. Above is a map of just one of them, at Modbury in Devon, which has the evocative name 'Runaway Lane', so called because this is where the Cavaliers were put to flight during the Civil War.

Canal towpaths in certain places have developed foliage on either side, which is sufficient to warrant their being known as modern green lanes.

LIGHT TRAFFI
ONLY

Chapter Eight

GREEN LANES IN TOMORROW'S LANDSCAPE

> There are only two real alternatives—to go on building new roads until the whole country is a concrete desert and we are all prisoners in our own vehicles, or to rethink the whole of our social organisation. The first solution is politically much easier, the second perhaps impossible to achieve in a democratic society.
>
> Christopher Taylor, *Roads and Tracks*, 1979

There has never been a time in history when the possibility of creating green lanes has been so great as it is now. As traffic becomes more concentrated on major motorways, the minor road network—at least in theory—receives less traffic; and because the upkeep of major roads and the creation of new ones absorb most of the funding available, lanes are the last in line to receive attention.

This is to their advantage, as nowadays they are created as a result of neglect. Once they have been neglected to a sufficient degree—with hedgerows overgrown, the road surface disintegrated, and water remaining as stagnant pools—paradoxically they become of value again. At this point their ruin becomes their rescue, and there emerges that fierce protective quality which the English feel for anything old. For those small groups of individuals who enjoy adopting lost causes, green lanes fit the bill.

As a result of the zeal and commitment of such groups, many green lanes have had their fate changed in an extraordinary way. Once they were the unlegislated major routes throughout England. Two thousand years later, parts of the Icknield Way, the Ridgeway and some Roman roads have become protected as public rights of way. And in this process they have, in a certain sense, become once again the most valued means of travel: for who, when given a choice between driving on the M25 and walking an old Roman Road, would not choose the latter?

Yet I know that there are those who are addicted to motorway travel, and in using the word 'addiction', all is explained. Britain has the greatest density of roads in the world, but we continue to build new ones—and to cut off sections of old ones which interfere with the passage of the new. We need to address the question of how green lanes will be treated in future highway and rights of way planning reviews.

If no longer maintained, in fifteen to twenty years a highway will become green; but its status is another matter. Present-day 'diversions' (a legal term denoting change of status) do not create green lanes in the grand manner of old drovers' or salters' routes; they only deal with short sections of road leading to and from busy highways.

As they will not form part of any future leisure route, their neglect will be of no great loss to walkers or cyclists. Two thousand years on, there is a clear case for preserving a section of a ridgeway or ancient causeway, but modern lanes only tell the story of England's precipitation towards gridlock. As such, can they be considered to have any value?

LEFT: Will this lane fall within the Ordnance Survey's new definition of "other routes with public access", or will it just disappear, either from lack of use or from over-use?

This alleyway once lead down to a thriving dockland area. It still remains untarmacked, and is a good example of an urban green lane with a history.

SAVING GREEN LANES WHICH REMAIN IN URBAN AREAS

This book cannot address the systemic problems that relate to road development, but I would like to suggest ways in which green lanes could be incorporated into any new thinking connected with plans to avoid 'carmageddon'. Many green lanes close to cities have been swallowed up by housing developments, obliterated in order to provide shopping facilities for the residents of these new settlements. People drive by car to these new shops. Surely it would be a good policy to try to incorporate these green lanes into plans for new housing, and to make them usable on foot and by bicycle? Some supermarkets, such as Safeways, now provide bicycle trailers for shoppers. Should any further supermarkets or other large stores need to be built, their position in regard to minor lane networks accessing new residential areas should be considered, instead of their being sited as close as possible to the nearest motorway. And if, in response to the widespread concern about the demise of local shops, any new shopping developments were on a relatively small scale—markets rather than supermarkets—minor green lanes could remain as their feeder roads, as they always have been.

This all goes hand-in-hand with the idea that suburban communities should take on a more human scale and be more self-reliant, instead of having the character of dormitory suburbs. A strong network of recreational paths would encourage this to happen: the communities would become more pleasant places in which to live. And indeed this is becoming the case in London, where a network of London Orbital Walks is being developed, which will eventually become known as the London Loop—a walker's answer to the M25. This system will incorporate many historic and beautiful green lanes.

The London Walking Forum, which has devised this network of orbital walks, is a partnership involving all the London Boroughs and those with voluntary recreational interests across London, including Countryside Management Services, the Ramblers Association, the Countryside Commission, the Sports Council, Lee Valley Park and the London Planning Advisory Committee. Its aim is to complete a 1,250 mile (2,000 km.) 'Walkers Web' by the year 2000: the London Outer Orbital Path and Capital Ring. Many of the green lanes involved in this will become incorporated into a system of maintenance, which is extremely important for their survival.

In the writing of this book I have included examples of many different types of green lane from all over the country. But Londoners can think themselves lucky, for

Examples of leaflets produced by local councils showing green lane walks, which are often part of national trails.

within this 'Walkers Web' there will be examples of all the periods covered in this history of green lanes, and nearly all the types of habitat through which they pass, with the exception of high moorland. In the Greater Manchester area and Bradford, problems of classification (see Appendix IV) are threatening green lanes.

At the time of writing, in early 1998, the Government is proposing to redevelop derelict inner city sites. This will mean there will be less encroachment on greenfield sites, and the idea of building on 'brownfield' sites (areas of industrial waste and derelict housing) will let many green lanes close to urban areas off the hook; let's hope that it happens.

THE FATE OF GREEN LANES IN THE COUNTRYSIDE

Firstly, there is some good news in respect of moorland green lanes, as the Ministry of Defence have just reissued their pamphlet entitled *Walks on Ministry of Defence Land*; there are ten walks featured, ranging over some of the 220,000 hectares of Ministry Land from Dartmoor to Castlelaw. But there is still controversy about access to these sites, especially around Otterburn and other areas. In the countryside, one of the main sources of recent green lane loss has been the new practice of discontinuing milk churn collections from the end of lanes: bulk tankers now go right down into farms,

Entrance to a green lane blocked by around ten years' uncontrolled growth of vegetation.

and as a result many of the the lanes have been tarmacked. Yet this is the working dimension of lanes which, as we have seen throughout this book, has usually been a crucial factor in their survival. We cannot complain too much about this practical use.

As we have seen, there are many examples of green lanes which form part of an ever-expanding network of national trails. The list is very long already, and there are more planned for the future. Here are just a few:

The Edward Thomas Trail (Oxfordshire and Gloucestershire).
The Severn Way (Worcestershire).
The Pennine Way.
The North Downs Way (from Farnham to Dover in Kent), which is 153 miles (245 km.) long.
The Icknield Way, (Bucks, Beds, Herts, Essex, Cambridgeshire, Norfolk and Suffolk), which is 120 miles (190 km.) long.
The Cleveland Way (from Helmsley to Filey Brigg), which is 120 miles (190 km.) long.

This is good news for green lane lovers, as it ensures their survival; and the mapping of such trails brings about attempts to show how they can be reached by public transport. The future of green lanes is inextricably interwoven with those of public transport and road maintenance: if we can mainly restrict the use of cars to main roads and motorways, the towns and countryside around them will be able to breathe more freely and take on a new lease of life.

As is widely acknowledged, we need recreation not only for our physical health but also for our mental well-being. The cycle path organisation Sustrans (Sustainable Transport) is a national body very much concerned with encouraging the greening of transport. The illustration below shows how green lanes have been incorporated into their system of cycle paths. Their aim is to create a network of cycle paths totalling 6,500 miles (10,500 km.), which will ensure that for at least twenty million people in the UK there will always be a cycle path within two miles of their homes. It is an ambitious yet workable

Part of the new Sustrans cycle path, called the West Country Way, from Padstow to Bristol.

Organisations such as the Youth Hostels Association often have their hostels placed along, or at the end of, a green lane.

project, which will benefit society on many levels. More people will be able to take exercise in safety (most of the paths incorporate disused railways or tow paths, or routes where the gradients are not too steep and are suitable to give access to all, including wheelchair users). The wildlife of the area will be protected and used as an educational resource, and there is also the prospect of creating five thousand jobs to maintain the cycle path route—presumably all these people will cycle to work! Sustrans has plans to link up with other cycle paths across Europe, thus promoting green tourism. Their latest path, the West Country Way, was opened in summer 1997. Connecting Padstow in Cornwall with Bristol, it is 250 miles (400 km.) long.

One of the particular problems in using green lanes as part of the recreational network is that often they exist as linear routes and cannot be incorporated into circular self-guided walks. But by taking them as they are, we acknowledge their historical significance: no one walked round and round in circles when going to work, and they never will!

Nowadays most county councils have Environmental Interpretation Officers who look into 'Access for All' to the countryside. Besides the making of maps, information boards and literature for various trails there are also guided walks which take you through green lanes in an 'interactive' way. But why? I think that meeting actors dressed as mediæval peasants along the way, or being robbed by a make-believe highwayman, is interesting and entertaining, but this is only one way of responding to the history present in a lane; there is also the physical evidence, and any documentary evidence waiting to be discovered or researched.

RECLASSIFICATION AS A FORM OF PROTECTION

The legal status of green lanes contains the key to their future. If a green lane currently categorized as an unclassified road is to receive any attention at all, it is best for it to be re-registered as a public right of way of some description. As a highway, it remains at the bottom of the pile, whereas as a public right of way it stands to receive attention from the relevant department of the highways authority, and also the possibility of being adopted by a voluntary body or the parish through which it runs. Some counties have developed a system of looking after their rights of way known as the Parish Paths Partnership Scheme: it works well within the framework of an environmentally aware local community. The best thing that can happen to a green lane which is at present registered as an unclassified road is that it becomes registered as a byway on the definitive map, and receives signposting and management through the Rights of Way department. This means that it becomes subject to what is known as a Definitive Map

Lawn or lane? This lane has been adopted—if not smothered—by a local conservation group. When maintaining green lanes, care should be taken not to completely destroy their natural appearance.

Modification Order (DMMO). At one time (when I worked for the MSC Green Lanes Project—see page 26), I believed that the reinstatement of the 'lengthman' would be possible. Lengthmen were once employed by county councils to maintain a particular area of a highway, and so got to know them in great detail. Unfortunately, funding for such employees is no longer available.

With recognition and signposting comes the danger of a lane becoming over-used, of frightening off the neighbouring wildlife and of causing erosion of the surface. Many counties have adopted a standard policy towards protecting their green lanes, one which embodies the principles of sustainable transport. Appendix III contains examples of policy statements taken from those counties which supplied me with information on what they consider to be the future of their green lanes.

Sometimes the fate of a green lane is such that it climbs up the highway hierarchy. Dodds, in his book *The Peakland Roads & Trackways*, says that sections of packhorse trails have been tarmacked in order to best maintain their surfaces, and packhorse bridges moved from main routes to minor ones, thus creating historical anomalies. Goyt's Bridge, in the Peak District, was moved a mile upstream from its original position in order to accommodate the Errwood Reservoir, in the process removing it from its historical context. But one should not be too picky about this, for after all most water conduits which once stood in the centres of towns and villages were moved to safer places with the coming of mains water supplies.

Then there are those green lanes which at present appear on maps as white ways. Some of these are privately owned, but how is the walker to know this? The Ordnance Survey are well aware of this problem and are at present collecting material from local authorities which will give them information on 'Other Routes with Public Access', to be defined as unclassified county roads and confined to rural areas. They will appear on OS 1:25000 maps as green dots and on the 1:50000 series as magenta dots. Many green lanes in rural areas will thus become identifiable to walkers, cyclists and horse riders. But there will be a caveat to their use, which relates to their legal status:

> The exact nature of the rights on these routes and the existence of any restrictions may be checked with the local highway authority. Alignments are based on the best information available.

This is further qualified when the OS show a topographic path or track:

> The representation on this map of any road track or path is no evidence of the existence of a ROW.

Some counties have already started to use this OS form of identification for green lanes, but the coverage has been patchy. In Devon, for example, only certain areas have been covered—I know this because I have been asked to survey the green lanes in the South Hams area of South Devon, so that they can be included in the manner suggested by the Ordnance Survey. You would be advised to check your own local OS maps for similar entries.

To sum up: local authorities have been obliged to reconsider the status of green lanes on two distinct occasions in recent times. Firstly, under the Highways Act of 1968, when RUPPs (Roads Used as Public Paths), were examined as to whether or not they should still remain in the highway system or be registered as rights of way. Secondly, the Wildlife and Countryside Act of 1981 asked authorities to look at green lanes and upgrade them or register them as BOATs (Byways Open to All Traffic). The latter, which goes hand in hand with the Definitive Map Review, should be completed by the year 2000, along with many other projected countryside projects such as Millennium Greens (village greens and green spaces in cities) and the London Loop mentioned above. They all involve complicated, expensive and lengthy processes of consultation with landowners, path users and other interested parties. But it is exciting to think that the Definitive Map reviews could change the face of the landscape for many years to come beyond the year 2000. Given the financial restrictions involved, we must not expect too much too soon.

USER GROUPS: CONFLICTING INTERESTS

Apart from changing status, another difficulty which affects the future of green lanes is the potential conflict between the various user groups, which may be placed in the following categories:

1. Walkers: both long distance, regular and occasional users.
2. Farmers and agriculturalists who use green lanes as access roads for their occupations.

LARA (LAND ACCESS & RECREATIONAL ASSOCIATION) CODE OF CONDUCT FOR THE USE OF GREEN LANES

1. Is it relevant? Restraint must be likely to solve a real problem.
2. Is it minimal? It must not extend beyond what is needed. If motorcycles, say, are not a problem, then do not include them.
3. Is it finite? The scheme can extend to three months, extendable for another three if real progress is being made and more time is seen to be needed.
4. Does it offer no threat even to hidden rights? Clearly it must be possible to claim later that because users stopped when asked they were obviously using the lane by permission.
5. Is the arrangement legal?
6. Are all relevant users also offering restraint? A problem of general overuse will not be resolved if only vehicle use ceases.
7. Do all local users within LARA agree? Compliance will be limited if users have no 'ownership' of the deal.
8. Is it user-led? One of the benefits of such a scheme is the publicity, locally and among user groups, arising from successful co-operative initiatives. This motivates users to obey signs and co-operate elsewhere.
9. Are there alternative routes? Neighbouring alternatives must be unobstructed and clearly available. In this regard 'a secret' unclassified road (UCR) is a poor alternative for a signed byway open to all traffic (BOAT).

3. Horse-riders.
4. Horse-and-carriage drivers.
5. Mountain bike riders and ordinary cyclists.
6. Motorcyclists and trial riders.
7. Four-wheel-drive vehicles.
8. Motorized vehicles using access roads for purposes other than occupational, e.g. tanks used in 'war games' routes.

Whether the LARA categorisation (see left) or any other is used, it can be seen that any exclusion of certain categories of users from green lanes has to be set out in a clear and logical manner. On the Ridgeway, a Code of Respect has been put up, which does not use judgmental language; yet it is precisely this lack of judgement which seems to upset different user groups! The Ramblers believe that what the Code of Respect says concerning the exclusion of motorized vehicles on many rights of way is right: it is right because they are right. They do not accept the premise that we all have a right to enjoy the countryside. Of course it is undeniable that those who do not drive cars or other vehicles along green lanes are inherently less destructive of the environment. Non-motorized transport users are saying that unless we respect the lanes' greenness we may destroy what at present we can all enjoy. Historically, these lanes are still in the horse and cart age, in 'The Landscape Changed' phase described in the previous chapter, but they are being used by vehicles which require a different kind of lane surface altogether. It is therefore important that codes of conduct be put in place.

I believe that where a lane can be proven to be of great historical importance, we need to go a little further than these voluntary codes of practice; that in itself will need clarification and further study.

In any event, there are going to be difficulties. If, for example, a bridleway is protected from being used by vehicular traffic, it needs to have a hunting gate which is wide enough for horses, but not four-wheeled traffic, to pass through. As mentioned in the previous chapter, these are sensitive matters which must be decided on a local basis. At Rosedale Chimney in Yorkshire (see page 104) there is a lane which was used on a regular basis for motorcycle scrambling until those taking part and the observers decided that the sport and road were becoming too dangerous; in this way unwritten voluntary restraint was exercised. A similar story can be told of the aptly named Corkscrew Hill in Cornworthy, Devon. It is therefore difficult to come to any general conclusions concerning how and by whom green lanes should be used in the future.

There are often protests arising from other kinds of use, such as a green lane being used to lead to a landfill site, or being used as a sewage disposal route. In these cases, the lanes are kept open and preserved in some way, although the reasons for this are not always compatible with what green lanes represent to the public. Nevertheless, a working lane is surely better than a neglected one.

In 1996 the Departments of Environment and Transport produced a consultation paper entitled 'Vehicles on Byways'. In its comments on the paper, the Council for the Protection of Rural England (CPRE) presents some frightening projections: for example, in its worst case scenario, over the next thirty years the traffic on country lanes will increase by an average of over 160%. In such circumstances, walkers, riders and cyclists who now use these lanes will be forced to use green lanes much more than they currently do. They suggest that a new category of ROW be created, which should be determined not only on the basis of the characteristics of the surface of the route, but also on environmental factors. They say that "these would need to be drawn up carefully to provide an additional 'sieve' through which proposals could be filtered."

They suggest that this new category be called Green Lanes, as this is a phrase which already has resonance with the public and which aptly portrays the character of many of these routes. They conclude that this new category should exclude rights of access by motorized vehicles.

The Automobile Association recently made a survey, entitled *Living with the Car*, which addresses the present day transport crisis. In the Road Management section they urge that 'walking and cycling be made easier for short journeys on local roads'. It seems that green lanes could form a large part of this network, and as such even the most habitual car user may consider their importance in the future. The RAC also have a policy of encouraging recreation in the countryside without motorized vehicles. There is hope that all users could co-exist, as they once did before motor cars became so universal—and universally destructive.

Any discussion about the use of green lanes must include the question of who controls their usage. This is the realm of the legal status of a lane, which we considered earlier in this chapter. It was seen that the legal and physical definitions of a green lane did not always coincide, so do we need to invent another status entirely?

THE CASE FOR A SPECIAL PROTECTED STATUS

Quite a lot of the research material sent to me by county councils for the purposes of this book came from their Registers of Ancient Sites and Monuments (RASM). Nottinghamshire, for example, said that they had forty-five historic sites called roads, eighteen called trackways and fifty-nine called holloways. But although they appeared in the list, they were not given any special protected status.

Chapter Three of this book, 'Building the Network', tells of how a particular lane in Suffolk was recognized by Hoskins as being ancient and in need of protection; today the county, because of lack of funds, is unable to carry this out. But it is also a matter of a lack of policy in regard to the preservation of ancient roads. Northamptonshire is at present in the process of designating part of Watling Street as an ancient monument which will be protected. There is a section of this Roman road which is at present a BOAT (Byway Open to All Traffic). The lane is extremely important in highway history terms, for not only does it show evidence of the Roman road fabric intact but it has some parts of the agger preserved and terracing in place. Three carriageways have been identified, at least two of which are Roman. Anglo-Saxon burials have been found along its length and it was used as a boundary road within this period. In mediæval times, the ridge and furrow pattern of fields came right up to its banks. The lane is in the process of receiving a Traffic Restriction Order (TRO), which will prevent any kind of four-wheeled vehicle from using it. Graham Cadman, from Northampton's Archæological Unit, also told me that a new status may be given to this historic road, in accordance with the rescheduling of ancient monuments which is being undertaken at present by National Heritage.

'Homes Fit for Heroes' was the slogan used after the First World War, promising housing for all. Although only forty years old, this disused green lane in Dunton Plotlands, Basildon, pre-dates the huge housing estate which lies next door to it.

When researching the Cheshire saltways, I wanted to know which sections had become rights of way, but no study to date has actually come up with this information.

RIGHT Children studying conservation and history in green lanes (top left); taking part in conservation work (top right); hands-on experience of road-making in the 18th century (bottom left); and taking part in a play called *The Lost Lane* (bottom right).

TOLL CHARGES
35 miles
Carriage with 5 horses
with 4 horses
with 3 horses
with 2 horses
with 1 horse

The course of this Surrey lane and its ancient hedgerow have been preserved so that all forms of transport may use it. But as the surface is now tarmacked, has it lost its 'green lane' status?

This green lane shows a tyring platform, once used by wheelwrights. The few remaining examples of this and other highway monuments could be preserved if legislation for the protection of lanes were more clear.

It is a time-consuming task, but it represents the kind of information which may be needed if any further rescheduling of roads as ancient monuments is to take place. Saltways are some of our oldest green lanes and certainly deserve protection, but there are others barely fifty years old which might require the same kind of attention. For example, there are the green roads which now run through Dunton Plotlands near Basildon in Essex, which mark the site of a development prior to the new town. As a modern reflection of the burgeoning interest in lost mediæval villages, Dunton should be recognized as a lost new town, and the lanes which still exist should be preserved.

The Countryside Commission have a scheme called the Countryside Stewardship Scheme. Partnerships are entered into with landowners, allowing access to their land by members of the public. Sometimes the access area may include an ancient earthwork or a field system, sometimes a green lane associated with these monuments, or just one which gives access to a farmer's land. Either way, grant aid is given to the landowner to maintain these lanes.

English Heritage's Monuments Protection Programme was originally set up to accelerate legislation to protect nationally important monuments: it ran from 1986 to 1996. Another aspect of its work was "to provide a comprehensive reassessment and a better understanding of the country's archæological resource, using a new classification system". Roads were included in this, and two studies have been made to date: one on Romano-British roads (1989), and another on mediæval roads (1990). Statutory protection is the next step in this process. As to their conservation, English Heritage states that for both kinds of road so far studied: "Where they occur they may be of little general conservation interest, but where they now exist as footpaths, bridle paths etc., archæological conservation may overlap with other management interests." This would seem to imply

A green lane with no signpost indicating its existence or status. At present we have to choose from: footpath, bridleway, BOAT, byway, RUPP, unadopted road, C road, D road, or unclassified road. In future all such lanes may be classified as Green Lanes, but such simplicity may be too much to hope for.

RIGHT

It is illegal to block a right of way or a public highway, yet many green lanes, because of their unclear status, are being blocked illegally by landowners (see above and left).

that green lanes which are not rights of way will not be protected by English Heritage unless they become part of the ROW network. I cannot completely agree with this approach, as I believe that certain ancient green lanes must be protected irrespective of their present day usage.

I also believe that there may be a case for preserving green lanes in a similar manner to the present Tree Preservation Orders—the old TPOs. These were set up under the Town and Country Planning Act of 1971 as being "expedient in the interest of amenity". If some lanes are to become rights of way, then they too need to be protected in the same way. The Dartington Institute study also recommended this approach, referring to Track Preservation Orders as TPOs (a new acronym would be needed in order to avoid confusion). The Hedgerow Regulations of June 1997, printed out in full in Chapter Five, provide a really useful practical guide to preserving the ancient hedgerows which are an essential feature of green lanes.

But what happens once the surfaces are tarmacked? Will they then lose their special protected status and be widened or bypassed as part of the development of adjacent highways and motorways?

THE NEED FOR EDUCATION

Many of us are familiar with the recent battle of Newbury and the Fairmile A30 protesters in Devon, but there are very few records of people taking up arms to protect an ancient road. This is, I believe, because of the lack of information and interest available. I have occasionally been approached by Devon County Council to give details on the history of lanes and to prove their age

In 1996 the artist Andy Goldsworthy was given a lottery grant to restore and redesign 100 metres of dry stone walls near Kirby Londsdale in Cumbria. The roads are still usable for driving sheep to indoor folds. RIGHT

so that they should not be incorporated into land which was being sold for housing development. But there is no national register of such lanes, nor organisation which looks out for them.

People occasionally spring into action when they see that a new road is about to ruin a local green lane network. This happened in Paignton, Devon, where the lanes associated with the writer Elizabeth Goudge were about to be swallowed up in a new bypass. The evidence put forward concerning the lanes' local and historic interest resulted in a deviation being made to the route. No doubt there are examples from other parts of the country: any local protest would be much more effective if, as in the case of listed buildings, a listed status were to be given to certain roads, so that they were protected from the beginning of the planning stage of development.

The people who now live in the shadow of new airport developments, such as those threatened at Manchester and Stansted, would surely be delighted if such a status were currently available for any green lanes which still exist near them. One of the most effective ways of protecting them is to tell others about them and to point out their historic and ecological value. This has proved a success in Devon, where the Manpower Services Commission Green Lanes Project ran for over five years. It surveyed, recorded, researched and restored the green lane network throughout the county. As part of the educational package associated with the scheme, I wrote a play called *The Lost Lane*, which was taken into nearly every school in Devon, of which there are over four hundred.

I have since had the pleasure of meeting former children who, having now grown up and become parents themselves, have passed on to their children the interest which was sparked off in them by school 'green lanes days'. Another project which has done much to encourage the recognition of green lanes is Common Ground's Parish Map scheme. Parishes are encouraged to record the historical and wildlife value of their area by making a map or document which will be available for generations to come.

As for the maintenance of lanes: this is something in which local groups can easily become involved, either through adopting a green lane and working to keep it passable or by bringing in a local wildlife trust or the British Trust for Conservation Volunteers to work on the lanes as a project. Other user groups will also contribute to maintaining an asset that it is in their interest to preserve. This has been the case with those who hunted in various areas in the countryside, but if things change in this regard, what will happen to the lanes they once used?

SETTING THE MATRIX: THE CASE FOR A NATIONAL REGISTER

The huge display boards, called matrices, which loom over motorway intersections and A-road junctions warn us of what is to come: they tell us about such things as lane and junction closures. The matrices are set from a computerized control room where the controllers are in possession of all the traffic facts. But if you are hoping to identify which white roads on the map are green lanes, and discover what they are like, you will not be given such clear-cut instructions about the nature of the problems you face: whether a 'stoggy', impassable morasse lies ahead; a landowner bars the way with a bale of hay; or a four-wheel-drive glee club is about to come round the corner and mow you down.

However, with the completion of the Definitive Map Review, many more green lanes will at least be signposted as ROWs, even though we cannot say what will become of them eventually.

Some counties and organisations are already very much aware of the value of green lanes. I quote in full from the study made by West Sussex:

> One purpose of the study is to discover and record one historic feature of the Sussex landscape which may be under threat because of current landscapes, brought about not by the natural forces of climate etc but by human economic activities. Although the country may not in general be threatened by the destructive road building programme that has seriously damaged all too numerous examples of ancient and unique landscapes (e.g. in Hampshire, Twyford Down?) is it not foresighted to recognise and record their particular landscape features before they are threatened and swept away without record.

Like other elements of the countryside, and particularly those that have changed as a result of human activity and the interactions of communities with their surroundings, green lanes are of interest to many different disciplines and fields of study, including historical geographers, ecologists and archæologists. These interests are over and above those of the general public.

Identifying green lanes, and attempting to discover something of their history, is a first step in providing for their future preservation and, if necessary, their management. It will also provide a badly needed database, which will foster an interest in this network of historical features and raise its profile in the consciousness of both the public and the planning authorities.

It is difficult to say just how such a register would operate, as the legal and physical definitions of any particular lane are often at odds with each other. The physical definition influences the lane's preservation, whereas the legal definition is primarily concerned with usage. For example, a lane with an unmade surface which is very muddy will quickly become eroded if used by all traffic, so should a restriction order of users be placed upon it? Or should it be tarmacked, thereby losing its green nature? My belief is that all lanes which fit the physical definition and have some historical or ecological value should be preserved, and their use by various groups should be monitored. This is already in place on the Ridgeway and on some stretches of Roman road.

Such an archive should be organized in chronological order (for example, all mediæval lanes in the country would be listed). It was not possible to compile such a register here (as some readers may have hoped for) because historical information needs to be obtained, collated and cross-referenced from many sources other than local highway authorities, who provided most of the information for this book. However, my hope is that this book will prove to be a catalyst, encouraging the many interested parties to pool their information and campaign for a national register of green lanes, before it is too late.

Once established, the kind of powers that a register would have—to protect green lanes and record their history, ecological value and possible future role in a Rights of Way network—remains to be discussed.

"RE-THINKING THE WHOLE OF OUR SOCIAL ORGANIZATION"

Christopher Taylor, one of the pioneer writers about road history, believes that this is what needs to happen if we are to save our landscape from further disintegration. One element in this re-thinking could be the planning of new towns so that they are car-free, and the incorporation of green lanes into new developments. Instead of whizzing off to superstores—although this will not be done away with completely—small corner shops could make a comeback, if prices were kept down and it was pleasant to walk or cycle to them along green lanes.

Even more significant in the design of future settlements will be that of changing work patterns. If present trends continue, more and more people will be working from home, linked to each other through the internet and maybe other new technologies, a scenario in which green lanes will surely become doubly important both for recreational purposes and as routes linking village to village. More locally based communities and economies could evolve, of which green lanes would be an important element. At present we 'travel without moving': we are no longer physically involved in the process of travel, and this is particularly true for journeys by car. Our travel mania reflects an unsatisfied inner need for 'real travel', a dissatisfaction which may account for many of the round-the-world epics by bicycle, on foot, by camel, on horseback and so on. And this is just where green lanes can step in—or we can step into them.

When you first picked up this book, you may have had a rather romantic view of green lanes. You may have thought of dappled, undisturbed cobbled paths where packhorses pecked away in slow progress up from the sea, laden with seaweed draped over hidden casks of rum. This is the image of the green lane which looks back to the past, going back into a world of leisurely, bucolic travel. Maybe you thought of green lanes as meandering over the landscape with no particular aim. Holiday routes, lazy days spent drifting through a green-tunnelled landscape. We think of those who used the lanes, and how we can seldom identify them; for lanes are not like houses which have been lived in for centuries and whose owners are recorded in the house deeds. A lane, though every bit as ancient, cannot list the wayfarers who trod its path over the centuries, so they must be almost entirely creations of our imaginations. Yet I hope that, having given examples from different periods of history, these travellers' costumes may at least be evoked as you follow in their footsteps. In looking back, we may find the way forward. By noticing these lanes in our landscape we will find a pattern and purpose in their existence, which will in turn convince us of the need to keep them preserved and used by generations to come. Whatever happens, they will always retain that sense of mystery which draws us to them in the first place.

> Two roads diverged in a wood, and I—
> I took the one less travelled by,
> And that has made all the difference.
>
> Robert Frost, *The Road Not Taken*

Before writing this book I realized that, in the main, people are only interested in what happens—or once happened—in a lane which they know personally. Yet it is of great importance that green lanes are now protected at a national level: a National Register for Green Lanes would be one such means of protecting them, and giving them the status mentioned at the beginning of this book, that of 'A Green Route Used Throughout History'. Such recognition at national level of their environmental and historical value will result in their continuing to be green for generations to come. It is up to all of us—working by ourselves, with conservation groups or with local councils—to find, and keep open, the green lanes of England which still exist in our own area, before they are bulldozed into oblivion.

Appendix I

HEDGEROW SURVEY FORM

Trees and woody shrubs in 30 paces: ______________________________
Left side: ______________________ **Right side:** ______________________
Evidence of bird and animal life: ______________________________

Trees	**Beg**		**End**	
	L	**R**	**L**	**R**
Ash				
Beech				
Birch				
Blackthorn				
Elder				
Elm				
Field Maple				
Gorse				
Hawthorn				
Hazel				
Holly				
Oak				
Privet				
Rose				
Rowan				
Sycamore				

Ferns	**Beg**		**End**	
	L	**R**	**L**	**R**
Black Spleenwort				
Bracken				
Broad Buckler				
Hard Fern				
Harts Tongue				
Lady Fern				
Maidenhair Spleenwort				
Male Fern				
Polypodium				
Soft Shield				

Flowers	**Beg**		**End**	
	L	**R**	**L**	**R**
Alexanders Arum				
Bedstraw				
Black Bryony				
Bluebell				
Bramble				
Campion				
Celandine				
Cleavers				
Cow Parsley				
Cranesbill				
Dandelion				
Dock				
Foxglove				
Ground Ivy				
Herb Robert				
Hogweed				
Honeysuckle				
Ivy				

Flowers	**Beg**		**End**	
	L	**R**	**L**	**R**
Knapweed				
Navelwort				
Nettle				
Plantain				
Primrose				
Speedwell				
Stitchwort				
Thistle				
Vetch				
Violet				
Yarrow				
Yellow Toadflax				
Willowherb				
Woundwort				

HISTORICAL INFORMATION

O.S. Sheet: ________ **Grid Ref:** ______________ **Dist:** ______________ **Parish:** ______________
Local name: ____________ **Official status:** ______________________________
Vantage points to: ______________________________
Historical / Archæological feature observed: ______________________________
Site: ____________ **Grid Ref:** ______________ **Sketch / Photo:** ______________
Place name evidence: ______________________________
Evidence of dating from hedgerows & banks: ______________________________
Evidence of lane being part of an ancient system of communication: ______________

Appendix II
DROVERS' ROUTES BY REGION

This Appendix lists, county by county, drovers' routes which survive as green lanes.

FROM WALES, THE WEST OF ENGLAND AND THE SOUTH

For the discoverer of green lanes, the routes which cross from England into Wales provide a rich hunting ground; indeed there are so many that there is a need for a separate study on border crossing lanes and the various purposes they have been used for over the centuries (see Bibliography).

Drovers approached England from Wales at three main points:

1. In the north from Caernarvon, Denbigh, Merioneth and Montgomery.
2. In central Wales from Powys by way of Abergavenny and Monmouth.
3. In the south via Newport and across the Severn estuary.

These were just the three main routes, upon which others converged. Examples of drovers' routes as green lanes for each of these regions can be found as follows:

1. The Golden Valley near Hay-on-Wye in Gloucester is a ridgeway, as is the Kerry Ridgeway, which starts at Radnorshire Gate near Dolfor and crosses the Kerry Hills to Bishop's Castle. Also in the north is the Portway, starting at Plowden (where the drovers would gather) and continuing through into Shrewsbury. It follows the route of the Long Mynd. The most northerly of these routes, which was known as the Welsh Road, came down from Wrexham.

2. The drovers who followed this central route would eventually link up with the Ridgeway in Berkshire. As well as going straight to London, cattle were sometimes driven from Anglesey to Kent.

3. One of the most southerly routes would cross at The Old Passage from Beachley to Aust and continue to Lechlade; it was also known as the Welsh Way. Liddington on the Ridgeway marks the point where the drovers joined.

The following is a listing of south-westerly counties that have green lanes today which once served as drovers' routes, linking up with traffic coming from Wales.

1. **Cornwall.** The existence of Hogs' Ways in this county, whence the animals were driven to Dorset and eastwards, contrasts sharply with the more ethereal Saint's Ways. Perhaps the only true examples of these are to be found along the sunken lanes which lead down to the Tamar estuary, the great divide between Devon and Cornwall which was eventually bridged by Brunel in 1851.

2. **Devon.** The so-called Abbot's Way, which links Buckland Abbey to Buckfastleigh, contains stretches of green lane which could have been used as cattle

droves. There is no reason to believe that a 'jobber' (the route is sometimes referred to as the Jobber's Way), was not dealing in the trading of cattle as well as tin. The existence of Erme Pound on Dartmoor indicates that there were routes along which the cattle were driven to be impounded, and then driven on and out to Green Hill. At Postbridge we find Drift Lane, running from the Archeton enclosures and up onto Broad Down; these are examples of transhumance or shieling lanes. Both Dartmoor and Exmoor also contain evidence of cattle driving in the form of clapper and packhorse bridges.

Besides London's central market at Smithfield ('smooth field') there were other centres in the south-west and east towards which cattle were driven or 'walked'. Because of the never-ceasing round of foreign wars during the seventeenth and eighteenth centuries, culminating in Waterloo, troops and seamen stationed on the coast required large quantities of salted beef.

In the years up to Waterloo (1812), five thousand cattle a year were slaughtered in Plymouth; eight years later this number had dropped to 700. Strangely enough, there are still some unmade roads surviving in the Bretonside area of the city on which may well have clattered the feet of cattle which provided the brawn with which to fight Boney (Napoleon).

3. **Somerset.** The areas around the Quantocks and the Mendips provided rich grazing grounds through which sheep were herded, as did those on Exmoor. Green lanes survive around the crossings which linked Wales with Somerset across the Severn at Beachley to Aust and Blackrock to Redwick.

4. **Dorset.** The Dorset Downs are obvious sheep-rearing country; many shepherds' routes linked up with drovers' routes which led further afield. In green lane terms this county had, in 1976, 140 miles (225 km.) of unsurfaced roads, the highest of any county in England. The majority of these are to be found in West Dorset.

Those on the Kimmeridge clay ridge, a dairy farming area, are numerous and short, whereas those on the chalk lands are long and sparse; these differences reflect different kinds of droving. The longest lanes are to be found in the parishes of Bridport, Compton Valence, Corscombe and Winterbourne Monkton. There is a lane called The Ox Drove at Berwick St John.

5. **Wiltshire.** Parts of the Ridgeway run through this county: as a long-established route, it was used by drovers coming from the south-west. Many green lanes once led to the big cattle fair at Weyhill, and pigs were driven eastwards from Beckhampton.

6. **Hampshire.** In defining the types of drove, many examples have been given of those which were particularly wide, thus giving plenty of room for the cattle to be driven up to ten abreast. The opposite kind of lane is the sunken one, which contained the livestock. The Harroway, which runs through part of Hampshire, was a route which stretched from Marazion in Cornwall to Dover through Salisbury Plain. It is prehistoric in origin but its use as a drovers' route can be clearly traced. There are trackways which connect the Harroway to the South Downs Way.

Another section of a drovers' route which follows a much older one is that known as the Old Way, and in certain sections as the Ox Drove, which runs from Walbury Camp to Basingstoke. There is evidence of a Saxon drove road running from Andover, a big market town, to Arlesford.

7. **Berkshire.** With entries into the home counties from the west, we reach the 'fattening fields' for some drovers' routes.

There is the Berkshire Ridge, sections of which were used by drovers, especially from the Goring Gap to Ashbury. Part of the Icknield Way also runs parallel to this route. It is from Berkshire that the snub-nosed black pigs came; they were bred here, stored in Oxfordshire and fattened in Buckinghamshire. In the middle ages Berkshire and the Cotswolds were great wool providers, so many of the green lanes remaining in the county date back to these times, having been used by sheep drovers to move the beasts on a local basis. There will be some green lanes (especially in Oxfordshire) along which cattle were driven to the Thames, for direct transportation by boat to London.

8. **Bedfordshire.** A mile before Totternhoe Camp on the Ridgeway there is an enclosure known as Maiden's Bower. Quantities of ox bones have been found here, which has been ascribed to the fact that the camp was a Roman fort; yet in Hippisley Cox's *Green Roads of England*, he refers to the drove road at Dunstable. It may be that this large quantity of bones is evidence of some disaster such as cattle murrain: that this is where the unfortunate beasts were disposed of, far from any town or the market which was to have been their destination.

9. **Surrey.** Old drovers' routes can be found along the long chalk ridges of the North Downs. Part of the Pilgrim's Way, which runs through this county, was a drovers' road. The direction of traffic, apart from local use, would have been towards London and to the November fair at Farnham, then on to Guildford over the Hog's Back.

10. **Sussex.** The dryness of the South Downs proved a problem for cattle drovers; this was solved by creating dew ponds, made by puddling chalk and clay and lining the pond with straw. The presence of these close to a green lane indicates its use as a drovers' way, whether short or long. In 1993 there was a study of the droveways in East Sussex between Bishopstone, an Archiepiscopal Manor, and Heathfield, its outlier (see Appendix IV).

This county prospered because of its wool trade; part of the South Downs Way, over its chalk downs, was undoubtedly used by drovers.

11. **Kent.** Although it is a long way from the central market of London, the naval town of Chatham would have received some traffic from drovers, as well as from the victualling yard at Deptford. In the Weald of Kent, the name 'droveden' or 'hollow way' is used, as cattle would have passed along these lanes.

OVER THE SCOTTISH BORDER INTO ENGLAND

The drove roads came from four main directions. Many of these ways coincided with routes from England into Scotland which were already in existence (see Chapter Two). An example is the Maiden Way—nothing to do with damsels in distress, but deriving from the Celtic 'Mai', meaning great, and 'Dun', meaning ridge. This was one of the main routes, over the hills down to Stanegate and then on to another section of Roman Road known as High Street.

From Dumfries and Lockerbie the drovers took routes across the Solway Firth to save them going back up country. There were obvious dangers in these crossings: here is a dramatic description from Samuel Smiles' biography of George Moore, written in 1878:

The sands were becoming softer. They crossed numberless pools of water. Then they saw the sea waves coming upon them. On! On! It was too late. The waves which sometimes rush up the Solway three feet abreast were driving in amongst the cattle. They were carried off their feet and took to swimming.

The most north-easterly drovers' way can be traced from the beginning of the Pennine Way, although not along all 250 miles (400 km.) of it.

THROUGH YORKSHIRE

After the great 'Tryst' at Falkirk, the drovers' ways would have divided in Yorkshire, according to whether they were heading for the markets of the Midlands and direct to London or making for the fattening fields of East Anglia.

Four main routes led through the Dales. The most obvious sections, still preserved as green lanes, are recorded here. They are joined along the way by other feeder lanes, some of which still remain green, but the main routes can be listed as follows:

1. Orton to Doncaster.
2. Kirkby Stephen to Wetherby and Doncaster.
3. Tan Hill to Wetherby and Doncaster.
4. Durham to York (the Hambleton Drove).

The famous fairs and cattle markets of Yorkshire make particularly interesting points of study, as many of them are not on main communication routes. Gearstones, famed for its corn and oatmeal market, the evocative-sounding Appletreeswick, and Malham Tarn in the Great Close.

One of the most famous Yorkshire drovers' routes is that now known as Hambleton Drove. This was an ancient lane which passed through such high places as Scarth Nick (a nick being a narrow passage through the mountains) and over Black Hambleton. It then splits near Steeple Cross, one road leading south to York and a south-easterly one making for Malton. Those heading along the latter were bound for the Wolds and the River Humber into Lincolnshire and the fattening lands of Norfolk.

Malton itself provides examples of drovers' routes dating back to 1230, when the Priory grazed their sheep, cattle and horses there. Dundale Pond must have been a stopping-off point for cattle through the ages; even today, common grazing rights at Levisham Moor are owned by twenty-six people, who can let out the grazing for over 2,000 sheep and a similar number of cattle.

THROUGH EAST ANGLIA TO LONDON

We are now entering the land of the 'droves', a word used to describe the wide roads through which the Scottish cattle passed on their way to markets and fattening lands in this part of the country.

It has already been noted how some parts of the Icknield Way were used for this purpose: a careful tracing of the route, using the Icknield Way Guides, will identify these (see Bibliography). The Peddar's Way, part of which runs along a Roman Road, was also used by drovers.

Drovers' routes which ran into the Midlands from East Anglia, and are of a later date, would have crossed into Banbury Lane between Northampton and Oxford before entering London from the west and north rather than from the north-east.

Sewestern Lane, also known as The Drift, runs from Harston (484800-332120) for 9.5 miles (15 km.) along the boundary between Leicestershire and Lincolnshire, to Thistleton (490240-318510).

One of the most famous fairs for cattle was St. Faith's near Norwich. At the height of the droving trade this was one of the most heavily populated areas of the country.

Just as the Hambleton Drove is famous as a Yorkshire drove road, I believe that the Grundle should be recorded as one of the most unusual drove roads in East Anglia. It appears today just outside the village of Stanton, at the end of Potter's Lane. Part of it has disappeared: it is now a footpath which leads down to what looks like a railway cutting. It is bridged at this point, and you can look down some twenty to thirty feet into a two-tiered lane. These kind of droveways were called grundles, the name referring to their gravel surface. There is another at Wattisfield, which has connections with the Roman pottery there.

Daniel Defoe writes of the driving of turkeys and geese from Suffolk into Essex; they would have come over the border at Stratford St. Mary on the long trek to Stratford atte Bowe, some miles further on. Also entering the county were cattle from Scotland and Wales, whose drovers would be looking for grazing grounds described by John Norden in 1594 as:

> the fattest of the lands, comparable to Palestine that flowed with milk and hunnye.

Appendix III

COMMENTS BY COUNTY COUNCILS ON THE FUTURE OF GREEN LANES

This Appendix comprises a summary of the replies by County Councils to the following question posed by the author in 1997:

> "Do you see any unclassified lane or group of lanes in your county being 'downgraded' in the near future?"

The purpose of the question was to determine how each county sees the future for those green lanes (sometimes unclassified roads) which are at present not within the Rights of Way system, and which Highways Departments in these counties are having difficulty maintaining. Many counties also gave information on the problems which these lanes face as a result of wear brought about by various categories of user.

BERKSHIRE

Berkshire follows the LARA guidelines laid out on page 120. The county favours a policy of voluntary constraint for four-wheel-drive users, but as this book is being compiled, moves are being made to ban them from those sections of the Ridgeway which run through Berkshire.

BUCKINGHAMSHIRE

The county has 134 unmetalled, unclassified roads on their register. They have been registered on the list of streets since 1954, but are gradually being eaten into by encroachments and other obstructions. In April 1997 steps were made to deal with this anomaly in a Draft Policy for Classification and Management of Unclassified Unmetalled Roads.

Voluntary agreements were sought between various motoring groups who all subscribe to the following Code of Conduct known as the four Ws.

> *Weather*
> Do not travel on green roads when they risk being damaged beyond a point of natural recovery when the weather improves.
>
> *Weight*
> Do not use lanes which may be serious damaged by the weight of your vehicle.
>
> *Width*
> Do not use lanes which are too narrow for your vehicle.
>
> *Winches*
> Use only when unavoidable and take great care not to damage trees, walls etc. while recovering.
>
> Remember that wildlife faces many threats and green lanes can be valuable habitats. Take special care in spring and early summer.

Buckinghamshire County Council states:

> In keeping with most counties, we find the most damage is caused to routes used by residents for access, agricultural damage is also significant, but generally little damage requiring repairs is caused by recreational use of vehicles on public rights of way.

Their policy for the future will fall into four sections. Firstly, they will seek to maintain the roads. Secondly, in consultation with LARA (Land Access and Recreational Association), they will enter into voluntary restraint agreements. Thirdly, where one and two above have failed, they may have to resort to a Traffic Regulation Order, but TROs are not to be recommended as they are costly (between £3,000-£5,000). The last resort would be a stopping-up order, which would cost even more.

An historical note here on stopping-up orders: Sidney and Beatrice Webb quote the following in their epic tome on highways, *English Local Government*.

> In a letter written in 1809 to the House of Commons committee on Broad Wheels and Turnpike Roads the following occurs:
> ....“any person who may possess only a few acres of land, and finds that the footpath in his neighbourhood either spoils the appearance of his grounds, or deprives him of that privacy he wishes, immediately proceeds barricading the said footpath: puts up a board, ‘No thoroughfare, Shut up by Order of the Justice, Shut up by Order of the Commissioners for Enclosing Waste Lands’ and such like intimidations, to the labouring peasant or artificer who by such artifices is forced out of the road.”

Things seem to have become worse than this as time went by and an act in 1815 for the Closing of Footpaths required just two JPs to close any footpath which they considered to be unnecessary, without any public consultation. A Hansard record of 1831 alleges that it was quite common for a Magistrate to invite a colleague to the following effect: “Come and dine with me, I shall expect you early as I want to close a footpath.” Such a lane was lost to the public in Wiltshire when in 1824 the Packway between Canon Frome and Ashperton was “diverted and turned and stopped up”, and the old highway reverted back to the owner.

Carriage drivers have been promised support by the county, as it is a very popular sport in the area.

CHESHIRE

In Cheshire there were originally about 200 RUPPs. The process of reclassifying them as BOATs, or more rarely footpaths, has begun. To date the process has only been completed in South Cheshire.

CUMBRIA AND WILTSHIRE

These two counties wish to establish a “collaborative approach” in the use of green lanes by four-wheel-drive vehicles: members of LARA have surveyed routes in the two counties and made their own recommendations as to what voluntary constraints on their use should be applied. Cumbria has become the subject of a Countryside Commission Demonstration Scheme in reducing traffic in busy areas. As a result a minor road at Loughrigg, popular with walkers and cyclists, has been signposted “access only” and motorized traffic reduced as a consequence. The green lanes which surround this area will also benefit from vehicle access having been moved further away from their habitats.

DERBYSHIRE

A reply came from the Rights of Way Review Officer who stated that no individual “unclassified lane”, or group thereof, was about to be downgraded.

ESSEX

Essex County Council produced a report on its protected lanes in 1974 (reprinted 1991). The county is well aware of the fact that “these lanes, with woodlands, are the main historic features which remain in much of the Essex landscape and there is a good case for treating them with a respect similar to that given to historic monuments, for this is what they are."

They adopt a similar approach to use and registration as outlined by Northampton. Their main enemy is the four-wheel-drivers. In the land of the boy racers, hunting gates and posts maybe the only answer to preventing them from churning up the roads.

KENT

John Whittington, the Countryside Projects Officer, sent details of how a thorough examination of every lane is being undertaken (see the entry for Kent in Appendix III). He states that the survey of the county's rural lane network has been completed, covering 2833 km. (1770 miles) of rural lanes, i.e. those roads which are class C or unclassified metalled roads.

District reports on the character and priority of protection, enhancement and restoration of these lanes are available for eight of the districts surveyed to date.

NORTHAMPTON

The county authorities believe that there are various ways of dealing with the problems of green lanes being misused, and of conflicting user groups.

When this becomes too much of a task they will bring in voluntary user groups to maintain lanes. They will then encourage user groups to exercise "voluntary constraint". After all these measures have been taken, should the lane still be misused they will impose restraints on vehicle access. Firstly, this will allow motorbikes to continue using them, but not four-wheel-drivers. If the lane is still unmaintainable, motorbikes will be prohibited as well.

NOTTINGHAMSHIRE

A reply was received from the Group Manager (Countryside) within the Planning and Economic Development Department. It stated that the green lanes in this county which are recorded as county maintained roads tend not to be "downgraded" as such. There are a number of such lanes which are either partly or wholly unsurfaced, and these are simply left unmaintained, or receive very little maintenance, in accordance with their minimal level of public use. A typical group of such lanes is located between Edingley and Halam at SK6553-6653 (Carver's Hollow: Wolfeley Hill Lane; Cutlersforth; Newhall Lane; Gray Lane).

With regard to the future of green lanes in Nottinghamshire, little change is expected in the existing situation. They extol the example given by Northumberland (see below) but regret that there are staffing implications in this which make it unlikely that it will be pursued.

NORTHUMBERLAND

Some unclassified county roads are being registered as Byways on the Definitive Map.

OXFORDSHIRE

Their Chief Engineer from Environmental Services stated that, because of current budget levels, all rural unclassified roads and most urban unclassified roads are not going to be maintained except for patching potholes. The consequence of this will be a gradual decline in the condition of many roads. There are no formal plans to downgrade roads; it is extremely difficult to do this in a structured way because of the near impossibility of declaring a road to be 'not required by the public'. The future envisaged is one of reluctant but necessary acceptance by the public of poorly maintained roads or, alternatively, more court appearances in which the county must defend itself against charges of non-maintenance of a public highway. It is not considered that there is any need to accept the downgrading of any lanes to green lane status: there are very few roads in the county that are little enough used to make this an acceptable option.

As for four-wheel-drive users, Oxford favours a policy of voluntary constraint as outlined above.

RUTLAND

The Director of Environmental Services stated that maintenance for unclassified highways will be subject to funding available.

The schedule is for rural unclassified roads to be surface dressed every eight years or so, which should be sufficient to extend the life of these roads indefinitely at current levels of vehicular usage. There are a number of green lanes within the County. Given normal usage (access for farmers to their fields, and occasional use for recreational activities by others, four-wheel-drive vehicles excepted), Rutland sees no reason why these lanes cannot continue in their present state for many years to come.

SOMERSET

Along with all other counties, Somerset is taking part in a review of the Definitive Map under the Wildlife and Countryside Act. This will be a complete survey and mapping of all public rights of way including applications for some green lanes to be upgraded or simply added to the map as Byways Open to All Traffic.

The Rights of Way Group added the following comments on the future of green lanes. The major problems as perceived by nearby landowners are twofold. Firstly, they fear the establishment of unauthorized travellers' camps and consequently seek to gate or obstruct formerly open lanes to prevent this. Their other concern, based on experience, is that there is unsuitable use by four-wheel-drive vehicles, which ruin the surface of the lane.

Unauthorized gating and obstructions are being used to counter this, together with applications under the 1981 Wildlife and Countryside Act for downgrading or deletion. Each application will be treated on its own merits.

SURREY

From the county's Rights of Way Group came a reply which stated that there were no plans to downgrade any unclassified lanes at present. It is proposed to use several BOATs as part of a Sustrans cycle network, whilst not, of course, excluding other users. There may well be more multi-purpose promotion in the future, with each case being looked at on its own merits.

Surrey has also been taking part in the Countryside Commission Demonstration Scheme outlined above (see Cumbria and Wiltshire). The Scheme has been implemented in south-west Waverley, an area of outstanding natural beauty (AONB); many roads have been protected for the use of walkers and cyclists only.

WILTSHIRE

See entry for Cumbria.

YORKSHIRE

Although no information was returned concerning the future of their green lanes, it is alarming to think of a town like Bradford not having a Definitive Map from which a record of lanes can be made.

CONCLUSION

During this century, local authorities have been obliged to reconsider the status of green lanes on two occasions. Firstly, under the Highways Act of 1968, RUPPs were examined as to whether or not they should still remain in the highway system or be registered as rights of way. Secondly, the Wildlife and Countryside Act of 1981 asks authorities to look at green lanes and upgrade them or register them as BOATs. The latter goes hand in hand with the Definitive Map Review and should be completed by the year 2000, along with many other projected countryside projects such as Millennium Greens and the London Loop mentioned in Chapter Seven. They all involve complicated lengthy processes of consultation with landowners, path users and other interested parties, in a series of expensive processes. It is exciting to think that the DMR will change the face of the landscape yet again. But will it only protect those green lanes which can afford it?

Ask this question of your local DMR officer and hope for a positive reply.

Appendix IV

IMPORTANT GREEN LANES NOT INCLUDED IN MAIN TEXT, BY COUNTY

Before writing this book, I contacted all the county councils in England and asked them to state which green lanes in their own counties they considered best represented the various historical periods that we have discussed. The response was patchy, but their comments heartening; most of the lanes they identified have been incorporated into the main text.

Below is a list of those counties which gave me information that has not been included above. I would like to take the opportunity to thank the counties and organisations who co-operated in this project, thus providing me with a basis from which to consider the subject. It must also be acknowledged that those counties who did not return information were not unwilling to do so, but merely lacked the necessary resources.

Remember that these are the lanes chosen by 'professionals'. You will probably have your own examples of green lanes which you know well, but you may not know about their status. It is a good idea to find out now, while the Definitive Map is being made. As a practical experiment in your own county, it would be a good idea to identify at least one green lane which best represents each of the different historical periods described in this book, and to make sure that it is going to be preserved—then go on to find many more miles of other examples.

BEDFORDSHIRE

The county provided information on the following periods:

Prehistoric

1. The Ridgeway from SP964448-TL003502. Forty Foot Lane from SP932596-SP980627 (part of this is a footpath only).

2. The Icknield Way. From TL085265-TL135301. This section is a green lane.

3. The Theed Way. This originally ran from Linslade in the west, but most of the route is no longer a ROW. The part that is a ROW has more the nature of a footpath than that of a green lane, but it is still a green lane from TL008264-TLO35259 and over the final section TL080265-TL085265, linking in with the Icknield Way at the latter point, as was the intention in prehistoric times.

Roman

Hassell's Hedge, from TL184493-TL198541, part of the Sandy to Godmanchester Roman road.

Anglo-Saxon

Yelnow Lane, from SP954597-SP977594. This could be Prehistoric or Anglo-Saxon.

Mediæval

Sweetbriar Lane TL129466-TL138445.

Green Lane TL226423-TL253418.

Totternhoe group of lanes around TL008214.

CAMBRIDGESHIRE

Although no information was received from the county, a study of its green lanes was made by Ruth Matthias in 1993, entitled *A Strategy for the Management and Protection of Green Lanes in Cambridgeshire* (unpublished diploma dissertation, Birkbeck College, London).

CHESHIRE

Information from the Public Rights of Way Unit stated that a quarter of the lanes in the county have been, or are being, reclassified. Examples of what they considered to be their best included the following (check with Cheshire ROW to confirm their present status).

Drovers' route

This is a salter's way running from Bank Lane at Jenkin's Chapel; an unclassified county road with a traffic regulation order on the central section. SJ972765 at the Cross to 984766 at the Church (Macclesfield and Alderley Edge).

Lambert's Lane, Congleton. First recorded in 1442. Now classified as Bridleway no. 1.

Parliamentary Enclosure Roads

In February 1997 this RUPP (number 19) was undergoing a change in status. It was proposed that it became a byway (check with the Department). It is to be found at Tushingham-cum-Grindley, and was set out in an Enclosure Award of 1795.

CLEVELAND (Hartlepool Borough Council)

Roman

Hutton Lane (NZ60601438-NZ60601404).

Mediæval

Gratham to Cowpen Bewley (NZ4827-4825).

In the district of Langbaurgh:

1. In the parish of Guisborough, Ruthergate Road (NZ60101550-NZ60401410).
2. In the parish of Guisborough, Godfalter Hill (NZ54481633).
3. In the parish of Skelton, Airyhill (NZ64901650-NZ72601930).

Drovers' route

Birk Brow to Commondale (NZ6598-1297).

CORNWALL

The counties of Cornwall, Dorset and Devon were not approached for specific green lanes information in the course of writing this book, in order to avoid giving the book too much of a West Country bias. It is generally known that this area of the country is rich in not-too-difficult-to-find green lanes. A Manpower Services Commission Green Lanes Project operated in East Cornwall in the 1980s, and a report on this should be available from the County Council. A book (by Liz Luck—see Bibliography) was also produced.

CUMBRIA

The Sites and Monuments Records office stated that they list drove roads, Roman roads etc., but they cannot check whether or not they fall into the category of green lanes or are in use as paved highways. They were kind enough to issue me with lists which give this information but are too long to be printed out here. Here are some of the definitions given for roads of historical importance: "holloways, trackways, roads, Enclosure roads, (dating from pre-Parliamentary Enclosure times as well), Drove roads, Roman roads, Corpse roads, Coal roads and Turnpike roads".

DERBYSHIRE

The Rights of Way Department states that the most important routes in the upland parts of Derbyshire, at least up till the development of the major turnpikes, were the many packhorse routes, the remnants of which are still to be found throughout the county. The most obvious route of this type which springs to mind is Doctors Gate, the reputed Roman road between Hope on the Sheffield side of the Pennine Hills over to Glossop on the western side (approximate grid ref. 171854-061947).

Drovers' route

The saltway through Longdendale (030977-156001), which was part of an ancient salters' route from Northwich in Cheshire eastwards over the Pennines. There appear to be 'green lane' sections of this which have been bypassed by the modern road.

Specific material relating to green lanes in the High Peak area of Derbyshire is available in the Dartington Institute Study, which stated that there are over a hundred lanes, amounting to over 150 miles (240 km.).

DEVON

See note under Cornwall. This area of the country is rich in green lanes that are fairly easy to find. In the South Hams area alone, the Dartington Institute Study recorded that there are over 500 lanes amounting to over 300 miles (480 km.).

The whole of the county was surveyed for green lanes in the 1980s during the course of the MSC Green Lanes Project. Detailed records of this, as well as a report, are available from Devon County Council.

DORSET

See note under Cornwall. Like Devon and Cornwall, this area of the country has many green lanes. In West Dorset alone the Dart Institute study recorded that there are over 600 green lanes amounting to nearly 400 miles (640 km.). It is best to apply directly to the Rights of Way department for details of lanes in any specific area.

DURHAM

This county has published many walks leaflets through its Environment Department, and inevitably there will be some stretches of green lane contained in individual walks. The Rights of Way department pointed out lead-mining trails which belong to the mediæval and industrial archæology periods.

ESSEX

I quote from a letter which explains their reluctance to point out any specific lanes. Given the threatened status of this county, because of its proximity to London, this attitude is thoroughly understandable (see Appendix III).

> If lanes became destinations instead of contributing to the experience of tranquillity enjoyed by those who venture into deepest Essex, their value in the landscape would be soon lost. The point of the policy is to fit traffic to the lanes and not lanes to the traffic, to save them from the 'improvement' which would be needed if they carried more vehicles.

GLOUCESTERSHIRE

This county publishes its own *Public Rights of Way and Conservation* Magazine which contains information on trails, such as the Gloucestershire Way, and ROWs which contain stretches of green lane.

HAMPSHIRE

The Planning Department of this county issues an excellent publication entitled *Ancient Lanes and Trackways*, many of which are green lanes. They also provided information on green lanes from various historical periods. A paper on the sunken lanes of East Hampshire has recently been written by Mr. J. Ockendon of East Hampshire District Council.

Prehistoric

The Harroway, parts of which run through Hampshire and once ran from Marazion in Cornwall to Dover via Salisbury Plain.

The South Downs Ridgeway between Kimbridge and Lomer and the South Hampshire Ridgeway.

The North Downs Trackway (Pilgrim's Way). This trackway consists of a ridgeway and lower terrace way. The term Pilgrim's Way has been attributed to the higher ridgeway, but really it should be included in this period as Canterbury Pilgrims used it well after its foundation years. There are also other green lanes which belong to this period, running as connectors between the Harroway and the South Downs Way.

Anglo-Saxon

The Cloven Way is supposedly the route taken by Cerdic and Cynric in the late fifth and early sixth centuries. The alignment runs between North and South Charford.

The Lunway, which is described as a true ridgeway. It begins in the old Saxon region west of the River Test, coming from Old Sarum by way of Lobscombe Corner. It reaches the Winchester to Basingstoke road at the Lunways Inn and is joined by a Saxon drove road from Andover to Alresford.

Mediæval

Part of The Old Way: Walbury Camp to Basingstoke (SU559550-564545).

Drovers' route

The Ox Drove (SU414589-428576).

National Trail

On The Isle of Wight a study was made in 1992 with the following title: *A site assessment and management plan for the Tennyson Trail Green Lane and Track on the Isle of Wight.*

HEREFORD AND WORCESTER

This is a region which contains a large number of green lanes and therefore, as with the West Country, further examples are not given here.

KENT

The council provided me with a plethora of information and pointed out that a list of the 'better' lanes which I required could run to over 5000 miles (8000 km.). I am listing below examples which show the detail included in their region-by-region Rural Lanes Studies. They issue a booklet which gives details of the trails and walks throughout the county.

Prehistoric

The 'Greenway' follows the foot of the Downs, following roads through Lenham and Charing Heath and on to Brabourne Lees and Stanford.

There are a number of ridgeways used by the Romans when they built their Roman roads, such as the road from Shore to Allhallows on the Hoo Penninsula.

Roman

Richborough to Dover and Canterbury to Beneden in the Weald are green lanes.

LANCASHIRE

The Pennine and Packhorse Trails Trust, based in Todmorden, is seeking to protect as many of these routes as possible. One of the ways in which they are doing this is by producing historical evidence to prove continuing usage of a lane. Their work is invaluable in that it makes people aware of our highway heritage and actively encourages them to save green lanes for future generations to enjoy as BOATs, wherever this is appropriate. The Trust also gave information on the existence of many green lanes in areas such as Calderdale, where lanes led from the industrial valleys up to the farming areas on higher ground.

LEICESTERSHIRE

Prehistoric

Salt Street and Roe House Lane. This runs from Norton Juxta Twycross (431300-306940) for two miles (3 km.) to No Man's Heath in Warwickshire (429040-308810).

The Drift and Sewstern Lane. From Harston (484800-332120) for nine miles (15 km.) along the boundary between Leicestershire and Lincolnshire to Thistleton (490240-318510).

Roman

Gartree Road forms part of the route from Leicester to Huntingdon, Cambridge and, eventually, Colchester. Burton Overy section from 467650-299480 for one mile to 469060-298690. Shangton to Glooston section from 471740-297160 for 1¾ miles (2.8 km.) to 474240-295780.

Part of the Fosse Way from Lincoln to Axmouth. From Stoney Bridge, Sapcote (450370-293000) for three miles (5 km.) to High Cross (Venonis), at junction with Watling Street (447240-288700).

Mediæval

Covert Lane and Coplow Lane.

From Scraptoft (464750-305520) via deserted mediæval village of Ingarsby, for four miles (6 km.) to Billesdon Coplow (470680-304880).

LINCOLNSHIRE

A study of the green lanes in this county was made in September 1990, entitled *Lincolnshire Green Lanes Project Report: September 1990*.

Prehistoric

See The Drift and Sewstern Lane under Leicestershire.

LONDON

As was mentioned in the final chapter, the London Walking Forum is involved in creating green walks round the city. The London Loop includes stretches of green lane within its 72-mile (115 km.) circuit, passing through many counties as well as Greater London. The circuit is divided into twenty-three sections. The Thames Path also includes green lanes within its length.

NORTHAMPTON & NOTTINGHAMSHIRE

The council provided me with information which in a few years' time could be expanded upon, once their computerized mapping system is in place. In addition, Northampton Leisure Services have a leaflet entitled *Roads and Trackways through the Ages*, a comprehensive survey which includes a map showing historic routes throughout the county.

Anglo-Saxon

A county and parish boundary which runs from the River Trent at Syerston (SK731492-SK795408) to the north-west of Bottesford was identified as being particularly important.

RUTLAND

Now once more a county in its own right, the following information came from the Libraries and Museums department.

Drovers' route

The most important one is Sewestern Lane, which starts in Rutland and stretches northwards into Lincolnshire. It is only green in parts.

Turnpikes

Some references to green lanes within the county are contained within *Turnpikes and Royal Mail of Rutland* (see Bibliography under letter 'R').

SHROPSHIRE

Drovers' route

The Kerry Ridgeway is a track which is reputed to have prehistoric origins but was also a drove road in the 18th and 19th centuries. It starts at Radnorshire Gate near Dalfor and crosses the Kerry Hills to Bishop's Castle. It is either a BOAT or a surfaced highway throughout this distance and is remarkable for its excellent views both northwards and southwards.

The Portway is a track which was certainly in use by drovers and others in the 18th century and may well have much earlier origins. It starts near Plowden, which was a gathering point for drovers, and follows the spine of the Long Mynd towards Shrewsbury. It is a bridleway or BOAT for most of its length and crosses a fine stretch of heather moorland owned by the National Trust.

STAFFORDSHIRE

Prehistoric

South of Wetton, Stable Lane (SK117540) passes several bronze age burial mounds including the unique Long Low and the Bincliff Lead Mines.

SUFFOLK

The Environment and Transport Department sent me a very useful printout from the County Sites and Monuments Record (SMR) which includes eighteen listed 'hollow ways'. Some of these are included in the main body of the book, but here is the complete list.

BRC / 001 / Med / 00791 / earthwork /moat / TL 895- 573-
BML / 016 / Un / 17191 / earthwork / ring ditch / TM 2982 5156
BUR / 005 / Med / 08348 / earthwork / moat , pottery / TM 0793 7565
CRE / 006 / Un / 03237 / earthwork / quarry / TM 222- 583-
EUN / 021 / Med / 15692 / earthwork / deserted village / TL 9100 7712
EXG / 058 / Med / 16070 / earthwork / deserted village / TL 623- 681-
HIG / 004 / Med / 06521 / earthwork / hollow way / TL 743- 655-
KTD / 010 / Un / 11505 / earthwork / road / TL 7040 6670
KBU / 005 / Med / 03220 / other structure / hollow way / TM 265- 598
LMD / 093 / Med / 15948 /documentary evidence / ancient woodland / TL 878- 481-
LMD / 094 / Med / 15949 / documentary evidence / ancient woodland / TL 890- 485-
MTT / 012 / Un / 15219 / cropmark / cropmark / TM 362- 898-
OTY / 025 / Med / 15804 / circumstantial evidence / moat / TM 213- 550-
STN / 037 / Un / 14291 / earthwork / hollow way / TL 8254 8427
SKT / 011 / Med / 05399 / excavation / moat, pottery / TM 0600 5760
TYY / 023 / Un / 16906 / earthwork / hollow way / TM 284- 372-
WFG / 023 / Un / 16343 / earthwork / hollow way / TL 9120 4355
WRE / 007 / Med / 01269 / earthwork / hollow way / TM 4885 8350

SURREY

Roman

The line of the road known as Stane Street is today represented by a green lane in the area between Dorking and Ashstead. The best stretch is known as Pebble Lane, and between the following grid references it is scheduled as an ancient monument (TQ180540-195568).

EAST SUSSEX

Roman

The Chalvington and Ripe Field systems still survive well and include green lanes, some of which joined the two systems.

Drovers' routes

The County Planning Department undertook a pilot study in 1993, looking at a series of droveways between Bishopstone, an Archiepiscopal Manor, and Heathfield, its outlier in the High Weald. As is so often the case, financial constraints meant that the study was never broadened, nor was the work published anywhere.

The county has developed a methodology used in the study, which is reproduced on page 152.

WEST SUSSEX

Within their general publications list and the South Downs Way, many of the routes described contain green lanes.

WARWICKSHIRE

There are two RUPPs in the County, and work on some 280 claimed (but not confirmed) BOATS has barely begun. Similarly, a study into the County Highway Record is proposed for later in the year; subsequently there will be a review of the Unclassified County Road network and its interface with the Definitive Map.

As you can see from the above, specific studies on green lanes on a county basis have been few. To date the following have been surveyed: Cambridgeshire, Cornwall, Devon, Dorset (Dartington Institute Study), the High Peak (Dartington Institute Study), Lincolnshire and East Sussex.

BIBLIOGRAPHY

The list below is by no means exhaustive: there are also many excellent local histories which need to be sifted through, to extract information on tracks and highways. A job for a National Register!

Albert, W., *The Turnpike Road System in England 1663-1840.* Cambridge. 1972.

Anderson, R.M.C., *The Roads of England.* 1932.

Barnes, B., *Passage Through Time.* Saddleworth, 1981.

Belloc, Hilaire, *The Old Road.* 1910.

Belloc, Hilaire, *The Stane Street.* 1913.

Belloc, Hilaire, *The Road* (Manchester). 1927.

Belsey, V.R., *Devon Roads Past and Present.* Past & Present Series, Silverlink, 1994.

Belsey, V.R., *Cornwall Roads Past and Present.* Silverlink, 1995.

Boyes, M. and Chester, H., *Great Walks: North York Moors.*

Beresford, M., *History on the Ground.* Sutton, 1957.

Blair, John, *Mediæval Surrey.* 1988.

Brandon, Peter, *The Sussex Countryside.* Hodder and Stoughton, 1974.

Bonser, K.J., *The Drovers.* 1970.

Brown and Fowler, *Early Land Allotment.* BAR, 1978.

Calvino, Italo, *Invisible Cities.* Harcourt Brace, 1972.

Cochrane, C., *The Lost Roads of Wessex.* Newton Abbot, 1969.

Copeland, J., *Roads and their Traffic: 1750-1850.* Newton Abbot.

Countryside Commission Pamphlet No. 186, *Out in the Country.*

Cossons, *The Turnpike Roads of Nottinghamshire.* 1934.

Crofts, J., *Packhorse, Waggon and Postland Carriage and Communications under the Tudors and Stuarts.* 1967.

Crosher, G.R., *Along the Cotswold Way.*

Dodd, A.E. and E. M., *Peakland Roads and Trackways.* Moorland Publishing, Ashbourne, 1974.

Drake, J., *The Motorways.* 1969.

Dunn, M., *Walking Ancient Trackways.* 1986.

Dyos, H.J., and Aldcroft, D.H., *British Transport: An Economic Survey from the Seventeenth Century to the 20th.* Leicester University Press, 1969.

Friend, John B., *Cattle of the World.* Blandford Press: 1978.

Fiennes, C., *The Illustrated Journeys of Celia Fiennes.* Ed. C. Morris, 1982.

Fuller, G.J., 1953. *The Development of Roads in the Surrey Sussex Weald and Coastlands between 1700 and 1900.*

Gregory, J.W., *The Story of the Road.* 1931.

Groves, R., *Roads and Tracks in Gill's Dartmoor: A New Study.* Newton Abbot.

Hawkins, M.R.H., *Devon Roads.* Devon Books. 1988.

Hemery, E., *Walking Dartmoor's Ancient Tracks.* 1986.

Hey, D., *Packmen, Carriers and Packhorse Roads; trade and communication in north Derbyshire and south Yorks.* Leicester University, Dept. of Communications, 1980.

Hindle, B.P., *Maps for Local History.* 1988.

Hindle, B.P., *Mediæval Roads.* Shire Publications, 1989.

Hindle, B.P., *Mediæval Town Plans.* Shire Publications, 1990.

Hindle, B.P., *Roads, Tracks and their Interpretation.* 1993.

Humble, Richard., *The Fall of Saxon England.* Book Club Associates,1975.

Hindley, G., *A History of Roads.* 1971.

Hippisley Cox, R., *The Green Roads of England.* 1927.

Hooke, D., *The Reconstruction of Ancient Routeways.* The Local Historian, 1977.

Hogg, *Inns and Villages of England.* Newnes, 1966.

Hoskins, W.G., *The Making of the English Landscape.* 1955.

Jackman, W.T., *The Development of Transportation in Modern England.* Cambridge, 1916.

Johnston, D.E., *Roman Roads in Britain.* Bourne End, 1979.

Jones, B. & Mattingly D., *An Atlas of Roman Britain.* 1900.

Jusserand, J.J., *English Wayfaring Life in the Middle Ages.* Fisher Unwin, 1889.

Kanefsky, *Devon Tollhouses.* Exeter Industrial Archæology Group.

Lincolnshire County Council, *Green Lanes Project report*. September 1990.
Lowe, M., *The Turnpike Trusts in Devon and their Roads*. Transactions of the Devonshire Association, December 1990.
Luck, Liz, *Green Lane Walks in South-East Cornwall*. Liskeard, Breton Press. 1985.
Mabey, R., *The Roadside Wildlife Book*. David and Charles, 1974.
Margary, I.D., *Roman Roads in Britain*. 1973.
Mingay, *Agricultural History of England from 1750-1850*. Volume 5 provided material for the Drovers and Packhorses chapter.
Pawson, E., *Transport and Economy: the Turnpike Roads of Eighteenth Century Britain*.
Peel, J.H.B., *Along the Green Roads of Britain*. 1976.
Pick, C., *Off the Motorway*. Cadogan and Century Books.
Reader, W.J., *Macadam*.
Roberts., *Translations of Stokenham Manorial Manor Rolls*.
Rowley, T., *Villages in the English Landscape*. 1987.
Rutland County Council, *Turnpikes and Royal Mail of Rutland*. Spiegl Press, 6, Georges Street, Stamford, Lincs.
Scott, Giles C.W., *The Road Goes On*. 1946.
Sheldon, G., *From Trackway to Turnpike* (East Devon). 1928.
Stewart, Gerry., 'Tracks, ways and Roman roads' in *Grassroots* magazine. Gloucestershire C.C. 1993-1995.
Stenton, *Anglo-Saxon England*. Oxford, 1971.
Strong, L.A.G., *The Rolling Road*. 1956.
Taylor, C., *Roads and Tracks of Britain*. Sutton, 1979.
Taylor, C., *Fields in the English Landscape*. Sutton, 1987.
Thomas, J.M., *Roads before the Railways, 1700-1851*. 1970.
Thomas, *Chronology of Devon's Bridges*. Transactions of the Devonshire Association. December 1992.
Toulson, S., *The Moors of the Southwest: Exploring the Ancient Tracks of Sedgemoor and Exmoor*.
Toulson, S., *The Moors of the Southwest 2: Exploring the Ancient Tracks of Dartmoor, Bodmin and Penwith*.
Toulson, S., *The Drovers*. Shire Publications, 1980.
Turner, M., *English Parliamentary Enclosure*. 1980.
Viatores, The: 1964. *Roman Roads of the South-East Midlands*.
Watkins, A., *The Old Straight Track*. 1925.
Webb, Sidney & Beatrice, *English Local Government, The Story of the King's Highway*. 1913.
Williams, Ralph Vaughan (Libretto by Harold Child), *Hugh the Drover*. Curwen Score, 1952.
Wright, G.N., *Turnpike Roads*. 1992.
Wright, G.N., *Roads and Trackways of the Yorkshire Dales*. Ashbourne. 1985.
Wright, G.N., *Roads and Trackways of Wessex*. Ashbourne. 1988.
Zuckermann, Wolfgang., *End of the Road, The World Car Crisis and How We Can Solve It*. Chelsea Green, White River Junction, 1991.

MAPS TO CONSULT

Ordnance Survey Maps

1924 Map of Roman Britain 1st Edition (2nd edition 1931, 3rd edition 1956).
1930 Seventeenth-Century England.
1932 Neolithic Wessex.
1935 Britain in the Dark Ages: South Sheet (2nd Ed. 1966).
1938 Britain in the Dark Ages: North Sheet.
1958 Monastic Britain.
1951 Ancient Britain (2nd edition 1964).
1954-5 Monastic Britain.
1962 Southern Britain in the Iron Age.
1974 Britain Before the Conquest.

Bodleian Map of Great Britain A.D. 1360 (The Gough Map).
Symonson's Map of Kent 1596.
County Records Offices will also have maps of the old turnpike routes.

The early OS two-and-a-half inch maps in your area are a good place to start when searching for Green Lanes, as are the six-inch OS maps, dating from the 1870s, which are available in Records Offices.

A METHODOLOGY FOR RESEARCH INTO GREEN LANES

The following is a summary of the methodology used by East Sussex County Council in one of their studies of green lanes. This may be useful to any organisation or individual wishing to make a similar study.

1. *Networking.* A list of useful contacts, both individual people and organisations.
2. *Library research and background reading.* See the Bibliography at the end of this book, and build up your own list of local publications.
3. *Definitive Rights Of Way maps.* The use of the Definitive Map provides a starting point for plotting roads that have been in use from time immemorial but are not "sealed against water" (i.e. tarmacked).
4. *Scanning aerial photographs.* Useful for recognising footpaths without boundary hedges.
5. *County Sites and Monuments Record (SMR).* Search for roads, tracks, holloways and linear features.
6. *Map regression.* Compare the 6-inch OS maps with the 1:10,000 maps, which show the definitive ROWs. This process will eliminate any very modern tracks.
7. *Fieldwork and recording.* Having completed the above stages, choose a pilot area and begin site visits.

GLOSSARY

Bavins: bunches of hard-wearing twigs, usually made of gorse or heather, used to absorb water and mud on rough road surfaces.
Causeway: a way which is raised above the level of the ground across which it travels.
Holloway or *hollow way:* a lane which sinks below the surface of the adjacent fields through which it travels.
Harrow way: this can be sunken, and is associated with military use.
Hundred: a land division originating in Saxon times and measured in 'hides', whose exact value varies from county to county.
Ridgeway: a route which passes over high ground, usually above a water course. Sometimes it follows this course from beginning to end.
Shieling: summer pasture on high ground.
Toll road: a road, usually across a landowner's property, for the use of which a fee was charged.
Transhumance: the movement of cattle from one area of grazing to another.
Turbury path: a way associated with peat production.
Turnpike road: mainly set up in the 18th century by groups of merchants, who charged travellers to use the roads which led from one market town to another.
Thane: an Anglo-Saxon lord.

CLASSIFICATION OF ROADS

footpath: access is allowed on foot only.
bridleway: access is allowed on foot, horseback or bicycle.
BOAT: Byway Open to All Traffic.
byway: same as *bridleway*.
DMR: The Definitive Map Review, which is to be completed by the year 2000, and which will list all public Rights Of Way on a county-by-county basis.
OS: The Ordnance Survey was established in the late eighteenth century to map out the land for military purposes. The OS maps are the definitive ones for use in any survey work.
permissive paths: Sometimes known as concessionary paths or bridleways, these are footpaths and bridleways where use is by permission of the landowner. However they carry no rights pertaining to ROW.
RUPP: Road Used as a Public Path.
PPP: Parish Paths Partnership.
PROW: Public Right of Way (same as ROW).
ROW: Right of Way.
unadopted road: not maintained by the highway authority.
unmetalled road: not tarmacked.

INDEX

The places and topics listed here are to be found in the main body of the text. Other place names and topics appear in the Appendices, which are arranged in order of county. References to illustrations and their captions are in **bold**.

Index

Index